Health & Safety
IN CARE HOMES

A PRACTICAL GUIDE

Sarah Tullett

ACE BOOKS

© 1996 Sarah Tullett
Published by Age Concern England
1268 London Road
London SW16 4ER

Editor Gillian Clarke
Design and production Eugenie Dodd Typographics
Copy preparation Vinnette Marshall
Printed in Great Britain by Bell & Bain Ltd, Glasgow

A catalogue record for this book is available from the British Library.

ISBN 0–86242–186–1

Contents

About the author

Sarah is a general health and safety specialist who has been actively involved in a variety of different aspects of occupational health and safety, particularly over the last twelve years. This has included experience in enforcement – working for a local borough council, a continuing publishing commitment with Croner Publications Ltd and the provision of information and the lobbying of appropriate bodies as the Engineering Employers' Federation's Health and Safety Adviser.

Sarah is currently Health and Safety Adviser to The Children's Trust, Tadworth, a charity that provides care, treatment and education to children with exceptional needs and profound disabilities. She is responsible for giving advice and developing policies on health and safety, food safety and fire safety for the departmental and line managers and the 400-plus staff and 150-plus volunteers.

Sarah is a firm believer in the current health and safety system and is keen to promote the benefits of good health and safety management. She also believes that health and safety should have a much higher profile and priority in schools and colleges in order to reduce the current level of ignorance of the subject in many workplaces.

Even in her spare time, health and safety is uppermost in Sarah's mind, as she dons appropriate protective gear every weekend to play goalkeeper for Horley Ladies Hockey team.

Acknowledgements

The writing of a book, no matter how familiar the subject, is always an exceptionally difficult task, which inevitably brings together a number of specialists and professionals. I am happy to acknowledge the contributions of the following people:

Kenneth Counder, Environmental Health Officer, Croydon

Geoff Driver, an independent registered safety practitioner

Stephen King, Personnel Health and Safety Consultants Ltd

Evelyn McEwen, Director of Information, Age Concern England
for reviewing the work and adding their comments and guidance;

Gillian Clarke for her editing of the material and for her enthusiasm
and patience;

The Children's Trust, for giving me the opportunity and experience to write this book and for their commitment and support throughout.

My sincere thanks to all of them and to everyone else involved in the project.

Sarah Tullett
June 1996

Introduction

Health and safety at work (occupational health and safety) is concerned with maintaining and improving the physical and mental well-being of employees at work and protecting anyone else who may be adversely affected by an employer's undertaking. Modern legislation lays down general principles that may be applied to all workplaces, regardless of the type of work carried out: it applies equally to offices, shops, factories, care homes, schools, hospitals so on. Some of the older, more prescriptive legislation is still in force, although it is being progressively repealed and replaced.

Care homes are therefore subject to the provisions of health and safety legislation, and managers, proprietors and employees all have defined duties to ensure the health and safety of themselves, staff, residents and any visitors such as contractors and residents' relatives.

The use of volunteer workers is commonplace in many care homes, and they provide valuable support for regular staff in the care of residents. Generally speaking, controls that are in place to ensure the health and safety of staff will be sufficient protection for volunteers performing the same work and tasks. This includes making sure that volunteers attend training courses relevant to their duties and that they are assessed to determine their ability to perform the required work safely. For the purposes of this book, 'staff' will be taken to include volunteers.

The very nature and purpose of care homes means that you, as owner and/or manager, will probably have to consider a wide range of work activities when fulfilling your legal duties. These activities may include nursing and other direct care work with the residents, catering, maintenance work, gardening, laundry, office work etc, and will be associated with such potential hazards as manual handling, electricity, equipment, infection control, medicines, gas and fire, to name but a few.

This book summarises the main legal duties, and provides more practical information to help you to comply with these duties. It is intended as a management aid, although it should also be relevant to staff who wish to know more about the subject.

The term 'care home' is used throughout the book for the sake of simplicity, and means both residential homes and nursing homes. Where there are differences, these are clearly defined. Similarly, there are references throughout the text to 'you' and 'your'; unless otherwise stated, these refer to the care home owner and/or manager. Terms that warrant fuller explanation are given in the Glossary at the end of the book.

The Health and Safety Executive (HSE) has published a guidance booklet HS(G)104 *Health and safety in residential care homes* (ISBN 0-7176-0673-2; £7.50), available from HSE Books (see p 176), which you are advised to obtain. The Department of Social Services publish *Homes are for Living* as well as issuing guidance derived from information provided by the Social Services Inspectorate, who have recently completed their review of the registration and inspection units throughout the country.

1 Health and safety at work

Health and safety at work is governed predominantly by the Health and Safety at Work etc Act 1974 (HASAWA), which imposes general duties on employers, employees and other specified people, and by many subsidiary Regulations which lay down detailed requirements in connection with specific hazards.

NOTE Health and safety laws are continually being updated and amended. This book includes existing amendments and discusses the laws as at the time of writing – but these may change during the life of the book. Where future amendments are known, reference is made to them. The original version of any law will *not* include or refer to subsequent amendments, which must be tracked down and read separately – your enforcing authority should be able to help you in this. You must keep up to date with any changes: ignorance is not a defence in the Courts.

The European Union (EU) is also an influential factor as the origin of much health and safety law in the UK. In addition to these statutory elements, there are recognised instances where it is possible to pursue certain actions (eg for personal injury sustained at work) through the civil, as opposed to the criminal, courts. These are discussed in detail later.

This chapter introduces the main duties under HASAWA, discusses the significance of the EU in UK national legislation and explains the role of civil actions in occupational health and safety.

HEALTH AND SAFETY AT WORK ACT 1974

This Act introduces basic ideas and principles to ensure health and safety at work and imposes specific duties on employers, employees, manufacturers and premises occupiers to achieve this.

Many, but not all, of the requirements of HASAWA are qualified by the phrase *'so far as is reasonably practicable'*. This means that you can balance the cost of correcting a hazard, in terms of time, effort and money, against the degree of risk posed by the hazard. If a hazard poses a significant risk (ie there is a likelihood of serious injury to one or more people) you will be required to do or spend more to control the hazard than if the risk is small or insignificant. A similar phrase, *'so far as is practicable'*, imposes a slightly stricter duty: you will have to do everything possible to avoid the risks in the light of current knowledge, technology and information – you are required to address foreseeable risks but will not be responsible for risks that are unpredictable or unknown at the time. This means that you are expected to keep up to date with current developments in your field of work and in health and safety generally. The strictest duties are *absolute* and require certain things to be done (or not done) regardless of the degree of risk and associated costs – these are usually written as *'shall'* or *'shall not'* in the legislation.

It is also important to understand that health and safety includes mental as well as physical health and well-being. This is illustrated by the increase in work-related stress conditions, which are now common occupational illnesses. It also includes welfare, so you must consider the provision of adequate facilities for staff: toilets, washing and changing areas etc (now covered by the Workplace (Health, Safety and Welfare) Regulations 1992).

Employers' duties to employees (section 2)

This is the most far reaching section and requires employers to ensure the health, safety and welfare of each employee at work, so far as is reasonably practicable. The very general and vague nature of this duty means that you should perform some sort of assessment of all your work activities and workplaces so that you are aware of any potentially dangerous situations that will need to be controlled. Details about risk assessment are given in the next chapter.

Section 2 continues with more detailed information on what you need to consider in connection with the general duty outlined above:

- Providing and maintaining safe equipment and systems of work.
- Ensuring that there are arrangements for the safe storage, use, handling and transport of articles and substances at work.
- Providing any information, instruction, training and supervision needed to enable employees to work in a safe and healthy manner.
- Maintaining the workplace and all entrances and exits in a condition that does not pose a risk to health and safety.
- Providing and maintaining a work environment that is safe and healthy and that has adequate welfare facilities.

You must also prepare, and when necessary review and revise, a written health and safety policy if you employ five or more employees. The policy should:

- acknowledge the existence of, and compliance with, HASAWA and all the other relevant legislation;
- demonstrate a commitment to maintaining and improving health and safety standards;
- detail the responsibilities for health and safety within your care home, including the limits associated with those responsibilities;
- define the arrangements for carrying out the policy – ie the safe working practices and procedures associated with your own particular work activities and environments.

Safety policies will be dealt with in more detail in the next chapter.

The remainder of section 2 is concerned with the appointment of, consultation, and other working arrangements associated with safety representatives from recognised trade unions. The Safety Representatives and Safety Committees Regulations 1977 (SI No 1977/500) provide for safety representatives to be appointed by trade unions recognised for collective bargaining/negotiating purposes. These safety representatives have the right to inspect the workplace, to see certain relevant documents and to investigate accidents at work. Employers must consult appointed representatives on matters of health and safety, and must allow them th resources to perform their safety duties, including attending training sessions, without detriment to their terms or conditions of work.

When two or more safety representatives request an employer to set up a safety committee, the employer must do this within three months. Such committees should have defined aims and objectives and consist of both employee and management members.

When there are no recognised trade unions, the employer does not have to appoint safety representatives or set up safety committees, but this may be worth considering even if staff don't request them: it may be an effective means of involving staff in health and safety.

New regulations, which will extend the right of consultation on health and safety matters to all staff, not just recognised trade union representatives, are expected towards the end of 1996.

Employers' duties to non-employees (section 3)

This duty is very similar to your general duty outlined in section 2. In section 3 the duty is to ensure the health and safety of anyone who may be adversely affected by your work – again, so far as is reasonably practicable. In practice this means that you have to have regard for anything in the course of the work carried out in the home which may give rise to any danger or harm to your residents, or to any visitors or contractors on your premises. This may include, for example, ensuring that all staff are trained to carry out manual handling techniques properly so that they do not endanger the residents by lifting them incorrectly, or ensuring that residents cannot gain access to floors that are wet and slippery. You must also assess the risks to your residents, so that the individual abilities of each resident to undertake certain activities are taken into consideration in determining the nature and degree of risk to them. It might be helpful to record these assessments in the residents' care plans.

With contractors, the contract should include a written declaration about health and safety and should specify the exact areas of responsibility (eg who is responsible for providing any equipment or substances that are required). You are entitled to see relevant health and safety documents the contractor's health and safety policy and the findings of their sessment.

This same duty also applies to self-employed people, who should work in such a way as to prevent any danger to themselves or to others who may be affected by their work.

Duties of premises occupiers (sections 4 and 5)

Section 4 applies to people who are not employers but who provide premises for use as a workplace or who provide equipment or substances for use in such premises; it is intended to cover situations in which employers cannot control the working conditions (eg in shared premises such as shopping malls). People in control of such premises should ensure that, for example, doors and windows and any common areas such as halls and stairs, and any equipment or substances, are safe and without risks to health. The duty is similar to that in section 3 and is probably not particularly relevant to care homes.

Section 5 requires people in control of premises to prevent the release of offensive or poisonous (noxious) substances into the air, or at least to render them harmless. This duty, which will soon be brought under the Environmental Protection Act 1990, is also unlikely to be relevant to care homes.

Duties on manufacturers and suppliers etc (section 6)

This section places various duties on manufacturers, suppliers, importers and installers. One duty is to provide health and safety information on any articles or substances supplied for use at work. Examples of these are the safety data sheets that should be provided with chemicals and substances supplied. If you order direct from a supplier the data sheets should automatically be provided with the substances ordered. However, if you purchase substances (eg cleaning agents) from a retail outlet, you will probably have to ask either the retailer or the manufacturer for the information, because retailers do not have to provide it even if the substances or articles are for use at work.

Manufacturers also have duties to carry out appropriate research and testing to ensure the safety of their products and must ensure, so far as is reasonably practicable, that the products are designed and constructed so as to be safe and free of risks to health when used properly. 'Used' is given its widest meaning and includes being set, used, cleaned or maintained in relation to articles (machinery), and used, handled, processed, stored or transported in relation to substances.

Employees' duties (section 7)

Section 7 places a duty on employees to ensure their own health and safety at work, and to ensure that their actions do not adversely affect anyone else. They must also co-operate with their employer in matters of health and safety.

Miscellaneous provisions

Section 8 makes it an offence to intentionally or recklessly interfere with anything provided in the interests of health and safety (eg to deliberately remove a machine guard).

Section 9 forbids employers to charge employees for any equipment or other items provided for the purpose of safeguarding health and safety.

Other sections cover the making of Regulations and approved codes of practice (ACOPs; see pp 17 and 173), issuing of enforcement notices for failing to comply with a legal duty and details of the offences under the Act, including offences committed by corporate bodies (eg the accountability of senior managers and company secretaries). Interpretations of terms used in the Act are given in sections 52 and 53.

ENFORCEMENT AND PENALTIES

HASAWA is enforced by one or other of two bodies, depending on the main activity or use of the premises. Health and Safety Executive (HSE) inspectors enforce the Act in industrial, factory-type premises, and local authority Environmental Health Officers (EHOs) enforce the Act in non-industrial premises such as offices and shops. Care homes are inspected by EHOs from the local authority where the home is situated.

Enforcement notices

An enforcement notice is issued by an EHO when there has been a failure to comply with any relevant law or when a serious incident is likely to occur. The two types of enforcement notice available to EHOs are *improvement notices* and *prohibition notices*.

Improvement notices

An improvement notice is issued when there has been a failure to comply with a legal duty. The notice will state what was wrong and what has to be put right, and by when this must be completed. The EHO does not have to provide guidance on what remedial action is necessary – only on what the end result should be.

A written explanation of what is wrong, what needs to be done and by when can now be requested before an improvement notice is served. The home then has two weeks to make representations to cancel or amend the notice. If no representations are made, the notice will be served.

Prohibition notices

A prohibition notice is issued when the EHO considers that there is a risk of serious personal injury. If this risk is considered to be imminent, the prohibition notice will be *immediate*. Otherwise, the activity giving rise to the risk must be stopped within a specified time – a *deferred prohibition notice*.

Prohibition notices can be issued against activities that are *about* to begin; there does not have to be an actual contravention of a legal duty – although, if there is, the notice must say so. Again, the necessary remedial action(s) need not be specified – only the required end result.

Appeals

It is possible to appeal to an Industrial Tribunal against an enforcement notice. Such an appeal must be made within 21 days. In the case of an improvement notice, the notice will be suspended immediately, until the result of the hearing. This is not so for prohibition notices, which continue to remain in effect.

The Industrial Tribunal will consider the enforcement notice and the appeal, and may:

■ cancel the enforcing notice;

■ confirm the enforcing notice;

■ require amendments to the notice.

Penalties

The Courts may impose considerable fines if an enforcing authority is successful in a prosecution. Health and safety prosecutions will always be heard at a magistrates' court (England and Wales) or a sheriff court (without a jury) (Scotland) in the first instance; if the case is not extremely serious, it will probably be dealt with by these courts. If a case is particularly serious, the magistrates' or sheriff court will refer it to the Crown court (England and Wales) or the High court or sheriff court (with a jury) (Scotland). It is possible in some cases for the defendant to request a jury trial at Crown court level.

The maximum fine available in magistrates' or sheriff courts is £20,000 per offence for failing to comply with sections 2 to 6 of HASAWA. At the Crown or High courts the fine is unlimited. In addition, if the offence relates to failing to comply with an enforcement notice or instruction or condition imposed by the courts, a six month prison sentence and/or the £20,000 fine may be imposed at the magistrates' or sheriff court level, or a two year prison sentence and/or unlimited fine at Crown or High court level. The other offences under HASAWA and the subsidiary Regulations carry a maximum fine of £5000 per offence at the lower level and unlimited fines at Crown or High court level.

NOTE These fines are set by legislation and are adjusted from time to time.

HEALTH AND SAFETY REGULATIONS, EC DIRECTIVES ETC

HASAWA lays down broad principles for ensuring standards of health and safety at work, and allows for the making of Regulations and approved codes of practice (ACOPs) to provide more detail in relation to specific hazards or work situations. For example, the Electricity at Work Regulations 1989 detail certain requirements, in addition to the general duties under HASAWA, to ensure that people are not exposed to danger by work with or near electricity; the Control of Substances Hazardous to Health Regulations 1994 (COSHH) detail certain requirements in relation to the use of harmful substances such as chemicals. The Health and Safety Commission (HSC) is responsible for the policy side of HASAWA (as opposed to the HSE who are involved in the enforcement side) and for drawing up and offering for consultation with all interested parties (including individuals) any new Regulations or ACOPs that may be required.

ACOPs are not legal documents although they define the minimum standards required by the legislation. It is not an offence to ignore an ACOP provided that the minimum standards are achieved by other means; if they are not, failure to follow an ACOP may be mentioned in any subsequent court proceedings.

The European Union (EU) is increasingly responsible for the health and safety legislation in the UK through the system of EC Directives agreed by the Member States; these have to be translated into national law within a given time. Negotiation on the contents of EC Directives is possible in the initial stages but, once a Directive is adopted, the provisions in it must be brought into effect in the Member States.

CIVIL LAW

In addition to HASAWA discussed above, it is possible for employees to bring civil cases against (to sue) their employer when they have been injured during the course of their employment. The Employers' Liability

(Compulsory Insurance) Act 1969 requires employers to take out insurance against any claims for damages awarded in civil court cases for personal injuries sustained at work. A certificate of insurance must be displayed at every workplace; failure to do so is punishable by a £400 fine.

Common law duties and negligence

Common law is the unwritten law of the land and basically imposes a duty of care on each of us towards everyone else. Any breach of this 'common law duty of care' forms the basis of negligence; this is now the most common route for seeking compensation in personal injury claims. Negligence cases generally consist of three parts:

- A general duty of care under common law to prevent foreseeable injuries.
- That common law duty is broken if someone acts negligently.
- The breach of that duty must cause the injury.

It is up to the plaintiff (the injured employee) to show that the employer was negligent.

Employers may be negligent by their own failings, through the failings of their management (in corporate bodies) or 'vicariously' through the failings of their employees. It is important to note that the duty of care is owed to employees individually and not collectively. This means that employers have a greater duty of care towards young or inexperienced people or people who may be particularly at risk in certain occupations (eg a pregnant woman carrying or moving heavy objects). The common law duty of care is not 'absolute'; that is, the employer is not expected to guarantee a complete absence of risks but must control them to acceptable levels. This is of course a similar duty to that imposed by section 2 of HASAWA.

Employees who caused or contributed to their injury (eg by not following defined systems of work) may be found 'contributorily negligent' and any damages awarded may be reduced accordingly.

Breach of a statutory duty

An employee may also sue an employer who has breached a legal duty. To win such a case, the employee must prove that they were personally covered by the legal duty, that the injury was of a kind that the legal duty was intended to prevent, that the employer breached this duty, and that the breach resulted in the injury. It is possible for breaches of legal duties to be taken through the criminal and the civil courts, but if both actions are successful, only one set of damages will be awarded. Again it is worth noting that some legislation (eg HASAWA, sections 2–8) and the 1992 'Management' Regulations do not allow breaches of their duties to be used in civil actions, except, with the 'Management' Regulations, in specified circumstances relating to pregnant workers.

NOTE The damages awarded in civil cases are usually considerably higher than fines imposed in the criminal courts, because they take into account loss of earnings, and pain and suffering. Two examples of personal injury awards include £42,000 to a worker who slipped and sustained a back injury during a manual handling activity, and £124,000 to a nurse who sustained a back injury while lifting a patient.

INFORMATION FOR EMPLOYEES

Section 2(2)(c) of HASAWA requires employers to provide any necessary information, instruction and training, so far as is reasonably practicable, to ensure the health and safety of employees. This requirement is repeated in many of the more specific Regulations made under the Act. In practice it is accepted that this information, instruction and training should deal with any hazards associated with the job and the necessary precautions to be taken.

Employers are also required (under the Health and Safety Information for Employees Regulations 1989) to display, in a prominent and accessible place, the approved poster 'Health and safety law – what you should know'. This poster summarises the provisions of HASAWA and has blank spaces to fill in with details of the health and safety enforcing authority for the care home and the local employment medical adviser (EMA) who will be located at the local HSE area office. Alternatively, the corresponding leaflet may be distributed to each employee. Copies of the poster or leaflets are available from HSE Books (see p 176).

KEY POINTS

- The Health and Safety at Work etc Act 1974 (HASAWA) is the main piece of health and safety legislation and lays down broad principles for ensuring health and safety at work. It is supported by Regulations which detail minimum standards for specific hazards. Older legislation, such as the Offices, Shops and Railway Premises Act 1963, is gradually being repealed and replaced, although some provisions are still in effect.

- HASAWA places duties on:

  employers to ensure the health and safety of employees at work and non-employees on the premises;

  self-employed people to ensure their own health and safety and to ensure that their actions do not adversely affect others;

  employees to ensure their own health and safety and to ensure that their actions do not adversely affect others;

  manufacturers and suppliers to ensure that their products or substances are safe when used properly and to provide relevant health and safety information about their products.

- HASAWA is enforced in care homes by local authority environmental health officers.

- The Act and the Regulations are criminal laws. Prosecutions for failing to comply with the law can be heard in the criminal courts, who have the authority to impose substantial fines or prison sentences, or both.

- Employees are entitled to sue their employers if they have been injured during the course of their work.

- Employers must display a certificate of employer's liability insurance.

- Employers must ensure that employees receive adequate and appropriate information, instruction and training to carry out their work safely. They must display the poster 'Health and safety law – what you should know' or distribute the corresponding leaflets.

Relevant guidance

L1 *A guide to the Health and Safety at Work etc Act 1974*

HSC13 *Health and safety regulation: a short guide* (free)

These are available from HSE Books (see p 176).

2 Health and safety management and risk assessment

Like any other area of a business, health and safety has to be managed, and, more importantly, needs to be considered as part of the business management as a whole.

Poor health and safety management costs employers vast sums of money every year, in many cases quite unnecessarily as the incidents that result in the losses are often preventable. This chapter looks at the main stages in health and safety management and discusses some of the most important features such as health and safety policies, arrangements for health and safety compliance, the appointment of 'competent persons' and the main tool in managing health and safety – risk assessments.

HEALTH AND SAFETY MANAGEMENT

Legislation

The Management of Health and Safety at Work Regulations 1992 (the 'Management' Regulations), as amended by the Management of Health and Safety at Work (Amendment) Regulations 1994 (the 'Amendment' Regulations), require employers to:

- carry out an assessment of the risks associated with their business, in order to determine how to prevent or protect against those risks;
- carry out measures necessary to prevent or protect against those risks;
- provide health checks to employees where appropriate;

- appoint 'competent persons' to help in meeting the relevant legal requirements;
- set up and maintain emergency procedures for dealing with serious and imminent danger;
- provide relevant health and safety information and training for employees;
- co-operate with other employers sharing the site;
- consider the capabilities of each individual to perform their work safely;
- ensure that temporary staff (eg casual workers) are informed of any health and safety information and/or skills necessary to do their jobs.

For most of these, the information must be kept in writing.

Employees have a duty to do their work according to the information, instruction or training provided by the employer, and to report any short-comings in the employer's arrangements for health and safety.

Where employees belong to recognised trade unions, employers must consult the unions and provide the necessary facilities and resources for the safety representatives.

The 1994 'Amendment' Regulations extend the requirement to carry out a risk assessment to include risks to new or expectant mothers (women who are pregnant, who have given birth within the last six months, or who are breast feeding). Other work or different working hours or even suspension are listed among ways of controlling the risks to their health and safety. A new or expectant mother who is suspended will still be paid unless she has refused suitable alternative work.

Practice

Five stages are recognised in managing health and safety: setting a health and safety policy, organising staff, planning and setting standards, measuring performance, and auditing, reviewing and revising these four stages, as necessary.

Health and safety policy

Section 2(3) of HASAWA requires anyone employing five or more people to have a written health and safety policy statement. This policy should show your commitment to obeying the relevant laws, define health and safety responsibilities throughout your organisation and contain details of the safe working practices your employees and others are expected to follow. The policy must be reviewed regularly and updated whenever there are changes to the work, equipment, procedures, etc.

Remember that health and safety policies are unique to each particular care home, so, although there will obviously be similarities, there will also be significant differences.

NOTE All the information that the 1992 'Management' Regulations require to be cross-referenced to, and linked with, the health and safety policy should be kept together.

Health and safety policies are generally accepted as consisting of three parts: the statement of intent; health and safety responsibilities; and safe working practices.

Statement of intent

This is your declaration and commitment to comply with all relevant health and safety legislation and to promote health and safety and good working practices throughout your home. It should be signed by the most senior manager – owner or chief executive – as a sign that health and safety is taken seriously at the highest level, and because such a person will have authority over staff and financial resources.

Health and safety responsibilities

This part of the policy should be clearly defined throughout your organisation, from the most senior manager downwards. Each staffing level (managers, supervisors, care assistants, etc) should have clear health and safety responsibilities, including any restrictions or limitations on these duties. If individuals have specific duties (eg manual handling advisers, safety representatives), these too should be clearly defined.

Safe working practices

These comprise the detailed part of the policy and should lay down the correct procedures to be followed for each work activity employees are required to carry out. Examples of the type of activities or areas that may need to be covered in care homes are:

- accident reporting
- assault
- blood-borne diseases (hepatitis B, HIV/AIDS)
- contractors
- drug abuse by staff
- electricity and electrical appliances
- fire procedures
- first-aid arrangements
- gas safety
- handling money/taking money to the bank
- hazardous substances
- infection (Legionella)
- lift safety – servicing and emergency evacuation in cases of power failure
- maintenance
- manual handling (people and objects)
- medicines (for residents)
- personal hygiene
- personal protective equipment (eg plastic gloves)
- residents (their welfare/rights)
- sharps (needlestick risks, broken glass, etc)
- smoking
- soiled linen/clothing
- stress
- work at height
- work carried out by someone on their own
- work environment
- work equipment.

NOTE   Further information on all of these subjects is given in other chapters in this book.

It is also important to consider how and where the activities are carried out; for example, moving or lifting residents is very different from moving or lifting catering stores. You may prefer to deal with each 'hazard' separately as in the list above and then just distribute the sections relevant to each employee's job. Alternatively, you may decide to prepare 'departmental' policies so that there is a policy for the kitchen, another for the care staff, and another for the gardeners and so on. In this case a lot of the information will probably be repeated in the different departments and just requires fine tuning, so you will not have to write new policies each time. Once the policy has been written, you must bring it to the attention of each employee either by giving them their own copies or by providing a central copy that is easily available to everyone.

Organising staff

Once the health and safety policy has been written, it must be put into practice – which requires the involvement and commitment of your staff. You need to develop a 'health and safety culture' within the workforce. Such a 'culture' will require you to deal with questions of competence, control, co-operation and communication.

Competence

Many Regulations require you to designate 'competent persons' for specific tasks, and in most cases this is accepted as someone who has the skills, training and experience necessary to perform the specific task safely and without risk to health. However, it is just as important to know an individual's limitations, as well as their abilities, so that their responsibilities do not exceed their level of competence. 'Competent persons' may be drawn from your staff but it may be necessary to seek outside expert advice in some cases.

The competence of staff is also important in ensuring that they are able to do their work safely and without risk to health. You must make sure your employees are given adequate information, instruction and training, and if necessary supervision, so that they understand the risks associated with their work and the precautions that must be taken to control those risks.

Control

Your health and safety policy will not run itself: to be effective, it will need to be controlled. This means that you will have to:

■ demonstrate your commitment to health and safety;

- identify areas where specialist advice is going to be necessary;
- ensure that everyone understands their responsibilities and knows that they may be accountable if something goes wrong.

If safe working practices are defined but are not being followed by a member of staff, you may have to set up disciplinary procedures to deal with the situation. You must first, of course, find out if there are any acceptable reasons why the safe working practices are not being followed, and this is where communication is so important.

Co-operation and communication

No health and safety initiatives will work unless they have everyone's support, so it is very important that you involve your staff. They should be consulted on all new developments, or in changes to existing practices, so that their knowledge of the work and environment can be taken into account. Not only will this increase their commitment to health and safety, but it will also ensure that such developments are workable and practicable, thus avoiding unnecessary waste of money, time and effort.

Even if your organisation does not recognise trade unions with designated safety representatives and safety committees, there is no reason why you cannot set up regular health and safety group meetings so that managers and other members of staff can discuss health and safety issues.

Planning and setting standards

Planning

Health and safety is not a once-only activity: your responsibilities do not end once you have written and implemented your health and safety policy. Health and safety is a particularly changeable subject and requires you to be proactive (see possible problems and prevent them) rather than reactive (eg investigating why an incident has occurred). You must cope with the ever-changing health and safety legislation which continually places different (if not new) duties on employers, and the technological developments to find safer machinery or substances etc. Your health and safety management system must reflect these changes and be able to respond to them.

Your health and safety plan should deal with hazard identification; risk assessment; control measures; compliance with legal duties; agreeing targets relating to health and safety for each of your departments; ensuring that health and safety is taken into account in all contracts; tasks, processes, equipment, products and services; safe work systems; co-operation between other employers and/or contractors on-site; and setting performance standards.

Setting standards

To be effective, you must define objectives for your health and safety policy, and set performance standards so that progress in achieving the objectives can be measured. The performance standards that you set must be measurable, achievable and realistic. Examples include defining an acceptable temperature range for the workplace – these may be different in different areas; and defining a training regimen for your employees, including induction and the frequency of refresher training and similar matters.

Measuring performance

This is basically comparing where you are now in terms of your health and safety objectives with where you should be. You should try to find out the reasons for any difference. Performance measurement consists of two parts: 'proactive monitoring' (undertaking regular inspections to ensure that the policy and safe working practices are being implemented and followed) and 'reactive monitoring' (assessing why an incident occurred and what lessons can be learnt from it).

Auditing, reviewing and revising

Unlike monitoring, which checks whether your health and safety policy is being carried out effectively, auditing should tell you whether your policy is achieving the desired results and, therefore, how reliable and effective your management system is. Monitoring and auditing should complement each other and allow you to see where there are any deficiencies in your management systems and where action is needed. Your health and safety policy should be reviewed regularly to take account of any changes or developments. When it is necessary to revise the policy, you should inform your staff of any changes.

RISK ASSESSMENT

Risk assessment is probably the most important tool in health and safety management. It has significant links with the health and safety policy, the arrangements for implementing control measures and the appointment of 'competent persons'.

Risk assessment is implied by section 2 of HASAWA, the aim being to ensure the health and safety of employees and others. Regulations that require risk assessment include the Management of Health and Safety at Work Regulations 1992 (as amended), the Control of Substances Hazardous to Health Regulations 1994 (COSHH) and the Manual Handling Operations Regulations 1992. Many more require that a form of risk assessment should be carried out in order to ensure that the product is suitable for the intended use and conditions; for example, the Personal Protective Equipment at Work Regulations 1992 and the Provision and Use of Work Equipment Regulations 1992.

NOTE If a risk assessment is required under specific legislation such as COSHH, you do not have to repeat it under more general legislation such as the 1992 'Management' Regulations, provided that your specific assessment is still valid and up to date. A record of the assessment (eg manual handling) may also be needed in the resident's care plan.

The principles of risk assessment are always the same: identifying hazard or hazards – including the people at risk from those hazards; evaluating the risk; and determining what control measures are needed. Risk assessments should look at the risks associated with *each* work activity, and should consider:

- work equipment used
- materials and substances used
- work environment where the activities are carried out
- people exposed, or likely to be exposed, to the risks
- organisational procedures (these will form the basis of your control measures).

Who should carry out the risk assessment

For the sake of consistency it is important that one person or a small team (eg the safety committee, if there is one) co-ordinates the risk assessment procedure. However, you may feel that your department managers should carry out their own risk assessments because they will have a thorough knowledge of the work and associated problems in their areas of responsibility. Under the 1992 'Management' Regulations you are required to appoint a 'competent person' to help you to meet your legal obligations and it makes sense that this 'competent person' should be involved in the risk assessments. You may feel that you do not have the required expertise in-house and that an outside consultant is required. Remember, though, that the consultant might not be familiar with your work or routines initially and will be making decisions on 'snapshot' pieces of information. It is very important therefore that the consultant has the opportunity to talk to your staff and, if necessary, the residents in order to get the maximum useful information.

Hazard identification

It is important to be clear about the difference between *hazard* and *risk*.

Hazard is the *potential* something has to cause harm; for example, a sealed bottle of bleach in a cupboard is hazardous – it has the potential to harm or cause damage but it is not a risk.

Risk is the *realisation* of that harm or damage actually occurring and takes into account the severity and likelihood of the outcome; for example, the bottle of bleach becomes a risk when it is opened and used.

Hazard identification is the systematic consideration of all the equipment, processes, activities etc associated with your work that may cause anyone personal injury or ill-health or that may cause damage to property. Below is a list of hazards that you may find useful as a means for deciding what hazards are associated with your particular home.

NOTE This list is not exhaustive and you may well have other hazards that need to be dealt with.

Hazard list

Hazards to employees

- manual handling
- assault
- hazardous substances (cleaning chemicals, pesticides, fertilisers etc)
- contact with soiled linen/clothing (biological hazard – exposure to biological agents)
- contact with blood and other body fluids (biological hazards)
- stress/depression (due to physical and emotional demands of the work)
- furniture and fittings
- work environment (temperature – too hot, too cold, too dry, too humid etc; insufficient work space, lighting levels)
- electrical appliances
- gas appliances (kitchen, room heating fires)
- stairs or other changes in floor level
- work equipment (hoists, machinery, tools)
- fire
- shift work and/or night work and/or long hours.

Hazards to residents

- medicines
- manual handling techniques by staff
- furniture and fittings
- changes to familiar layouts (eg moving furniture around)
- stairs or other changes in floor level
- slippery, uneven or cluttered floors
- fire (eg residents who smoke, portable fires)
- lack of appropriate supervision or monitoring (scalding hot water in baths, excessive freedom for residents who are unable to take full and proper care of themselves)
- abuse by staff (verbal and/or physical)
- transporation by vehicle.

Your risk assessment should also deal with hazards associated with non-routine work such as building maintenance, and any social activities such as a barbecue or outings arranged for the residents. Contractors and other visitors may be exposed to any of the hazards listed above depending on the terms of the contract, where relevant, and their actions while on the premises.

Remember to take into account different circumstances in which similar work is done – for example, during a day shift and during a night shift. The control measures may well be different. Do not overlook the very simple and obvious hazards: night staff may have to move about in reduced light, and a simple, effective control measure would be to provide them with torches. Risk assessments must be regularly reviewed and revised to take account of changing conditions, such as pregnancy – findings at the beginning of pregnancy may not be valid at the end because of the physiological changes that occur.

Risk evaluation

Once all the hazards have been identified it is necessary to decide whether they are potentially a 'high', 'medium' or 'low' risk to the people exposed. This risk rating is completely arbitrary, must be suited to your own special circumstances, and will depend to a large extent on your existing control measures.

Risk evaluation must take into account the likelihood of the harm or damage actually occurring and the severity of the outcome if it does. At its simplest, 'high', 'medium' or 'low' ratings may be given to the hazards identified, although it is possible for numerical values to be assigned to both the likelihood and the severity factors; these can then be multiplied together to give a priority value for each hazard – see the example below. You can devise your own system, there is no right or wrong way to evaluate risks; it is a question of personal preference, although it is important that the same person is involved in the evaluations in order to achieve some kind of consistency during the risk assessment.

The risk evaluation must be considered for the employees and residents as individuals. For example, pregnant women are likely to be more at risk from manual handling activities during the later stages of pregnancy than when they are not pregnant. The suitability of the work for the individual is an important point to remember – fitting the job to the person not the person to the job is sound advice. A frail resident is more at risk than one who is fairly mobile.

Risk assessment example

This simplified example is designed to illustrate the risk assessment process for a common work activity in care homes – laundry. It is only a guide and is not a substitute for your own risk assessment.

Step 1: Identify the hazards

The hazards (things that have the potential to cause harm) that you may reasonably expect to find in laundry areas are:

- Dangerous machinery – washing machines, dryers, garment presses
- Exposure to hazardous substances:
    - chemicals such as cleaning agents, detergents
    - biological agents such as contact with soiled linen or clothing
- Slippery floors
- Electricity – especially in a wet environment
- Manual handling – lifting and carrying linen
- Work environment – hot, humid, poor ventilation
- Poor posture – bending over sluice sinks, ironing boards at the incorrect height
- Fire

Step 2: Identify who is, or is likely to be, exposed to the hazards

You should concentrate first on controlling the risks that affect most people. The people who may be affected by the hazards listed above are:

- Staff working in the laundry
- Staff carrying items to and from the laundry
- People servicing or maintaining the equipment
- Refuse collectors
- Visitors to the laundry.

Step 3: Evaluate the risk associated with each hazard

In order to carry out this step you need to consider what control measures you already have in place and how effective they are. Remember that *risk* takes into account the 'likelihood' and 'severity' of the outcome. Some control measures that are applicable to laundries are:

General measures applicable to all hazards

- Training
- Provision of information
- Defined and known safe working practices/safety policy
- Supervision

Specific measures

- Interlock door safety devices – to prevent doors being opened while the machine is in use
- Planned preventative maintenance programmes for equipment and regular servicing
- Thermostatic controls on heat-generating equipment
- Selection of 'suitable' equipment (ie suitable for the intended use and intended place of use)
- Height-adjustable ironing boards
- Adequate ventilation
- Electrical safety devices – correct fuse rating, residual circuit breakers, positioning of sockets away from water sources, etc
- Provision of trolleys to move laundry around
- Breaks away from boring work/job rotation
- Personal protective equipment (PPE).

All the above information is put together so that a risk evaluation can be made. The hazard of electricity will be used to demonstrate the three risk-evaluation methods discussed above: (1) assigning 'high', 'medium' and 'low' ratings; (2) assigning numerical values; and (3) using a risk evaluation matrix. Method 2 allows a more detailed evaluation of risk than method 1, and method 3 is more detailed than method 2.

Assigning high, medium and low risk ratings

This is the simplest method and is based on your judgement as to whether the hazard poses a high, medium or low risk.

Electrical equipment in an environment where water is present is a potentially lethal situation. If there were no control measures in place, the risk would be 'high' because of the likelihood of a severe injury. Likely control measures are:

- ensuring that the equipment is suitable for the job you intend it to do and the environment you intend to use it in;
- only trained and authorised staff may use the equipment, and they are familiar with the associated risks and correct procedures for use;
- the presence of electrical safety devices such as fuses, earthing, residual circuit breakers;
- an effective planned preventative maintenance programme.

By implementing these control measures the likelihood of an accident occurring is reduced, although, in this case, the severity may not be. This would then warrant a 'medium risk' rating.

This process should then be repeated for each of the hazards listed above so that a clear hierarchy of control priorities is achieved for the laundry. The hazards with 'high risk' ratings should be your top priority and dealt with first.

The drawback with this system is that it does not directly take into account the likelihood and severity factors that determine a risk value: it looks at the situation as a whole. On the other hand, it is simple to understand and to implement.

Assigning numerical values

This system gives greater flexibility in determining your control priorities, which are worked out on *final* numerical scores obtained by multiplying together the individual values assigned to the 'likelihood' and 'severity' factors. In this example the values for 'likelihood' and 'severity' are:

Likelihood	Severity
Very likely to occur = 3	Death or major injury = 3
May occur = 2	Minor injury = 2
Unlikely to occur = 1	Non-injury = 1

If no control measures are in place, an incident could be expected to be 'very likely to occur' and to cause 'death or a major injury': it would get a $3 \times 3 = 9$ rating. As control measures are introduced, both the likelihood and the severity should be reduced to a 'may occur' and 'minor injury' level: it would get a $2 \times 2 = 4$ rating. These risk ratings define clear control priorities as follows:

$3 \times 3 = 9$ high risk/high control priority

$3 \times 2 = 6$ high risk/high control priority

$2 \times 2 = 4$ medium risk/medium control priority

$1 \times 3 = 3$ medium risk/medium control priority
(because of severity of outcome)

$2 \times 1 = 2$ medium risk/medium control priority

$1 \times 1 = 1$ low risk/low control priority – but do not ignore

Once this procedure has been completed for each hazard, you will have a clear priority hierarchy for introducing controls where they are needed most.

High, medium and low risk matrix

This method allows an even greater definition of risk values, and the risk evaluation and control priorities are worked out using a grid matrix incorporating vertical 'likelihood' and 'severity' axes with directly linked high, medium and low ratings along each.

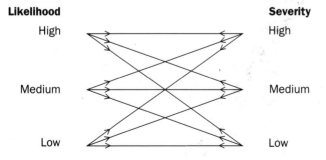

The possible combinations from this matrix are:

Likelihood		Severity		Risk/Control priority
High	×	High	=	High
High	×	Medium	=	High
High	×	Low	=	Medium
Medium	×	High	=	High
Medium	×	Medium	=	Medium
Medium	×	Low	=	Medium
Low	×	High	=	Medium
Low	×	Medium	=	Low
Low	×	Low	=	Low

Step 4: Control measures

Once the risks have been evaluated, you should have a clear idea of which ones you need to deal with most urgently. The high risk situations will require urgent attention and should be addressed first, the medium risks next and low risks last. A hazard with a low risk rating cannot be ignored – it still must be considered and controlled.

Ideally, risks should be eliminated whenever possible, or, if this is not possible, adequately controlled. Personal protective equipment, including clothing, should be provided only as a last resort if the risks cannot be controlled by other means. (See Chapter 3 for more information on accident control hierarchies.)

The examples given here are completely arbitrary and are used to illustrate the risk assessment process. You should follow a risk assessment system that suits you and your home. Experiment first with the different systems by assessing the risk posed by a particular hazard so you can get a direct comparison. As long as hazards are identified, risks evaluated and effective control measures implemented, you are fulfilling your legal obligations. Remember that the significant findings of your risk assessment must be recorded if you employ five or more staff: you may find it useful to record the risk assessment anyway for future reference when you come to review it at a later date.

Determination of control measures

By now you will know which risks to tackle first: those that are likely to occur and/or that are likely to have a severe outcome. The control measures that you already have in place will influence the risk evaluation, which should then highlight areas where extra measures are needed to prevent or at least control the risks to acceptable levels.

Help in defining the necessary control measures can often be found in official guidance, either from the HSE or from professional bodies. Sometimes the required levels of control are defined in legislation (eg many hazardous chemicals have exposure limits that are specified in the Regulations and are legally binding). There is also a recognised order of priority for control measures, which is discussed in detail in the next chapter. Basically, you should look to prevent or eliminate a risk; if this is not possible, you should reduce the risk to the lowest practicable level and in any case below any limits required by law.

Control measures include practical items such as hoists to eliminate or reduce the need for staff to lift residents, or local exhaust ventilation and extraction systems to remove harmful dusts and fumes, and cleaning/gritting pathways to prevent their becoming slippery with leaves or ice; even the use of warning signs is a control measure (though it is of limited value with confused or mentally frail residents). Factors such as training and the provision of information and instruction in how to carry out the work safely also count as control measures, as does planned maintenance (equipment that is maintained well and regularly is less of a risk than equipment that is allowed to operate until it breaks down). Likewise, the provision of adequate supervision, monitoring and other health and safety arrangements are all acceptable control measures, and will reduce the level of risk, as will the appropriate use of safety signs and signals (specified under the Health and Safety (Safety Signs and Signals) Regulations 1996). Personal protective equipment (PPE) (eg plastic gloves) is also an acceptable control measure, although this should be used only if the risks cannot be controlled by other means.

Records, review and revision

Your risk assessment must be reviewed regularly to ensure that it reflects the current work situation. If changes have occurred in, say, the work activities or equipment, the assessment should be revised to take these changes into account. The 1992 'Management' Regulations require the significant findings of the risk assessment to be recorded if you have five or more employees but it may be useful to keep a note of all your findings, regardless of the number of your employees.

Relationship with health and safety policy

The health and safety policy should reflect the findings of your risk assessment and then define the safe working procedures necessary to prevent or control the hazards identified. There should be adequate cross-referencing between the two. Likewise, the risk assessments required under more specific legislation (see p 21) should be appropriately cross-referenced to the general risk assessment so that an enforcing officer and anyone else can easily see what risks are associated with the work. You must also carry out the control measures that have been determined by the risk assessment; again, it is good practice to keep a record of these, and to review them regularly.

KEY POINTS

- The Management of Health and Safety at Work Regulations 1992 contain various provisions relating to managing health and safety, including the important provision of requiring a risk assessment to be carried out.

- In addition to the legal requirements, there are recognised stages in implementing an effective health and safety management system; these include setting a policy, organising employees, planning and setting standards, measuring performance, and auditing and reviewing the previous stages.

- A written health and safety policy is also required under section 2(3) of HASAWA. This should contain a statement of intent to comply with legal duties, define health and safety responsibilities throughout the organisation, and lay down clear, detailed, safe working practices for each work activity.

- The risk assessment should consist of hazard identification, risk evaluation and control measures for each work activity.

Relevant guidance

L21 *Management of Health and Safety at Work Regulations 1992 – ACOP*

HS(G)65 *Successful health and safety management*

IND(G)132L *Five steps to successful health and safety management – special help for directors and managers* (free)

IND(G)133L *Selecting a health and safety consultancy* (free)

IND(G)163L *Five steps to risk assessment* (free)

Writing your health and safety policy statement: guide to preparing a safety policy statement for a small business

All the above are available from HSE Books (see p 176).

3 Accident prevention and accident reporting

By definition, accidents are unplanned events which may, but need not, lead to personal injury and/or property or other damage. HSE figures for 1994/95 show that the most common work accidents relate to manual handling activities, falls from height and slips, trips and falls on the same level. All of these are possible in a care home. Figures for 1990 indicate that accidents at work cost UK employers between £4.5 and £9.5 billion per year, while the costs of individual accidents range between £90 and £200, or between £170 and £360 per employee. In most of the cases making up these figures the initial accident resulting in the loss could have been prevented.

Many factors contribute to the total costs of accidents, including such obvious ones as insurance premiums, fines and legal fees and personal injury awards. There are, however, other aspects that are less obvious but which can have a devastating effect on the business. These include costs related to reduction in productivity, retraining/rehabilitating injured staff or recruiting replacement staff, the accident investigation and associated paperwork/administration. Another important factor is the loss of goodwill and reputation, which may lead to bad publicity, which in turn could affect the confidence of your clients, or potential clients, and in your ability to attract new staff.

This chapter looks at ways of preventing accidents, and then explains your obligations under certain legislation to report and/or record accidents on your premises.

ACCIDENT PREVENTION

To a large extent your risk assessment will provide the basis for your accident prevention programme by identifying the most significant hazards associated with your work and considering the effectiveness of existing control measures. Details contained in 'accident books' or other records also provide valuable information on the types of accidents or incidents occurring within the home, and will allow you to define trends – whether a certain type of accident is common in a certain area, whether people working night shifts are more accident prone than day staff, and so on. All of this will be useful for helping you set your priorities for action.

Accident theory and investigation

Various research projects over recent years have confirmed that there are recognisable ratios between different accident types. Research suggests that, for every one fatal accident, there are 30 serious injury accidents and 300 non-injury or property-damage-only accidents. Controlling these 'minor' accidents is therefore cost-effective and should prevent a more serious accident occurring in the future. All accidents and incidents should be investigated as soon as possible after the event and the details recorded. This means, in practice, that there must be systems in place to ensure that all accidents are reported to management, and that subsequent investigations are carried out. Even 'near miss' accidents that do not actually result in any harm or damage must be investigated because these can highlight shortcomings in your procedures and management systems before a major accident occurs.

Accident control hierarchy

Although it is impossible to detail ways of preventing all accidents that might occur in each care home, there is an agreed hierarchy of control measures that you should take into account:

■ eliminate the source of danger (eg avoid or stop the activity)

■ substitute for the hazardous process or substance etc one that is less hazardous

■ provide appropriate engineering controls (eg hoists for lifting residents)

■ reduce the number of people exposed to the danger

- reduce the duration of exposure
- provide adequate information, instruction and training to enable employees to work safely
- provide personal protective equipment (PPE) – as a last resort to protect people at risk.

Not all of these will be applicable to your care home, although they should provide a sound basis for controlling accidents.

ACCIDENT REPORTING

Accident reporting is required under two sets of Regulations: the Reporting of Injuries, Diseases and Dangerous Occurrences Regulations 1995 (RIDDOR) and the Social Security (Claims and Payments) Regulations 1979.

Reporting of Injuries, Diseases and Dangerous Occurrences Regulations 1995

RIDDOR requires a responsible person, usually the employer, to report to their health and safety enforcement authority (the local authority environmental health officer) the accidents and dangerous occurrences listed in the Regulations. Note that acts of physical violence are included in the definition of 'accident'. The injuries or incidents of relevance to staff in care homes that must be reported include:

- fatalities;
- all fractures except those of the fingers, thumbs or toes;
- all amputations;
- dislocation of the spine, knee, hip or shoulder;
- loss of eye, or chemical burns/penetrating injuries to the eye;
- injuries requiring immediate medical attention or resulting in loss of consciousness due to an electric shock;
- loss of consciousness due to lack of oxygen;
- certain poisonings or infections resulting in acute illness or loss of consciousness;

- any injury resulting in hypothermia, heat-induced illness, unconsciousness, or requiring resuscitation;
- any injury resulting in immediate hospitalisation for more than 24 hours;
- injuries that result in four or more consecutive days off any work that might reasonably be expected to be carried out by the injured person whether or not it is part of their normal duties. (When calculating the number of days, the day of the accident is excluded but you should take into account Saturdays and Sundays even if these are not normally worked.)

In all the above cases, except the 'over three day' injuries, the environmental health officer (EHO) must be informed immediately by telephone and a written report must be submitted within ten days. With regard to 'over three day' injury accidents the EHO must be informed in writing within ten days.

Workplace accidents that result in the hospitalisation or death of a resident must also be reported under RIDDOR.

There is an official form (F2508, available from HSE Books) which may be filled in and submitted; you do not have to use these forms provided that you give all the required information. You must also keep a record of any reported accidents; the record must be kept for three years from the date on which it was made and contain the following information:

- the date, time and location of the accident;
- the name and occupation of the injured employee or, if not an employee, name and status (eg resident, visitor);
- the nature of the injury, and a short description of the circumstances;
- the date on which the incident was first reported to the EHO;
- the method by which the incident was reported (telephone, writing).

Keeping a photocopy of any RIDDOR reports sent to the EHO is accepted as sufficient evidence of compliance with this requirement. In certain situations the EHO is entitled to ask for further information about the incident reported.

RIDDOR also requires certain dangerous occurrences and occupational diseases (listed in the Regulations and the accompanying guidance document) to be reported. Most of these tend to relate to industry as opposed to the care service but, for example, hepatitis may be contracted through work involving exposure to human blood products, secretions or excretions. There is an official form (F2508A) for reporting the disease, which must be reported as soon as the employer receives the medical diagnosis of the condition and the work relates to that specified in the Regulations. Records about an occupational disease should contain the following information:

- the date the disease was diagnosed;
- the name and occupation of the affected person;
- the name or nature of the disease;
- the date on which the disease was first reported to the EHO;
- the method by which the disease was reported (telephone, writing).

Social Security (Claims and Payments) Regulations 1979

These Regulations require you to record all injury accidents (regardless of how trivial they seem) that occur in your care home. The Regulations apply if you employ 10 or more staff, although it is good practice to keep such records even if you have fewer staff. The records are required if an employee claims Social Security benefits because of an injury sustained at work. The information that you must keep is:

- the name, address and occupation of the injured person;
- the date and time of the accident;
- the location of the accident;
- the cause and nature of the injury;
- the name (and certain other details) of any person (other than the injured person) who records the injury.

There is an officially published 'accident book' (BI 510, available from HMSO; see p 176) for recording the information but, again, you do not have to use this if you have a record of the required information. The 'accident book' must be kept for three years from the date of the last entry and be retained in a central location on the premises. The information contained in an 'accident book' will be useful in highlighting accident trends in your home and in supplementing the information required under RIDDOR. It will also be a useful document for your insurers in the event of a civil claim (eg for personal injury sustained at work – see 'Civil law' on p 17).

Your health and safety policy should define the procedures for reporting accidents in your home.

KEY POINTS

- There are considerable financial and other benefits to be gained from preventing accidents at work.
- The most common accidents are related to manual handling activities, falls from height and slips, trips and falls on the same level. With good proactive health and safety management systems, most of these accidents are preventable.
- Certain injuries are required to be reported to the enforcing authority (the EHO) under the Reporting of Injuries, Diseases and Dangerous Occurrences Regulations 1995.
- All accidents must be recorded in an 'accident book' or equivalent form under the Social Security (Claims and Payments) Regulations 1979.
- Accident statistics are an extremely useful source of information when implementing or reviewing accident prevention programmes.

Relevant guidance

L73 *Guide to the Reporting of Injuries, Diseases and Dangerous Occurrences Regulations 1995*

HS(G)96 *The costs of accidents at work*

HS(G)155 *Slips and trips*

HSE31 *Everyone's guide to RIDDOR 95* (single copies free)

All the above are available from HSE Books (see p 176).

4 Workplaces

One of the factors that you are required to consider under section 2(2) of HASAWA, in order to fulfil your duty to ensure the health, safety and welfare of employees, is the actual workplace where they are expected to work. Although care homes are 'home' for the residents and therefore very domestic in their nature, they are also workplaces for the people who care for the residents, whether as carers or in a support service, and so are subject to certain legal requirements. It is a question of finding the correct balance between obeying the law and having an informal, homely atmosphere.

The Workplace (Health, Safety and Welfare) Regulations 1992 expand on this general provision and cover specifically the physical work environment such as:

- temperature, ventilation, lighting;
- the way in and out of the place of work;
- staircases and other structural aspects;
- housekeeping such as cleaning (including the safe cleaning of windows), maintenance, disposal of refuse;
- welfare facilities such as toilet, washing and rest facilities, and changing accommodation.

Many of the points covered by the Regulations will almost certainly have been addressed in ensuring the safety and comfort of the residents. This chapter discusses the various factors involved in ensuring a safe and healthy workplace in care homes.

PHYSICAL WORK ENVIRONMENT

Temperature

The workplace temperature should be reasonable, which is defined as being a minimum of 16°C. If the work is physically strenuous, a minimum of 13°C is considered reasonable. In care homes these minimum temperatures are unlikely to cause many problems, given that the home will probably be kept at a comfortable temperature for the residents. Indeed, the problem is more likely to be that the temperatures are too high to carry out work activities comfortably and you will need to consider effective means of ventilation.

No maximum temperatures are specified for workplaces, so it is a matter of judgement and personal preference as to what constitutes an acceptable upper temperature. The most obvious area where this may be a problem is in the kitchens, which generate a considerable amount of heat from the ovens and stoves. Again, it is important to ensure that there is adequate and effective ventilation/extraction in these areas. Staff must be able to take breaks away from the hot areas, and there should be drinks to replace lost body fluids. Dehydration and heat fatigue/stress in hot work environments may significantly affect the ability of an employee to work safely, especially where dangerous machinery is used (eg meat slicers).

You must also consider and deal with the effects of adverse temperatures on anyone working outside (eg gardeners) – see also Chapter 9, Personal protective equipment.

Ventilation

All enclosed workplaces must be ventilated with fresh or purified air. This may mean, at the simplest level, opening windows, or, in more complex situations, providing extraction systems for the kitchens, or air conditioning plant.

Lighting

All workplaces must be adequately lit, preferably by natural light. Where necessary for reasons of health and safety, there must be appropriate emergency lighting in case a work area could become unsafe if the artificial lighting failed. It is possible that the level of lighting will be determined to some extent by the needs of the residents in order for them to move around safely. Certainly a good level of lighting is required on stairs and other places where there is a change in floor level, where furniture and other items have to be navigated and also where detailed or delicate work is carried on (eg in maintenance workshop areas). Consideration should also be given to the effects of lighting on computer screens to prevent glare and reflection.

Lighting controls should be positioned or protected so that they are not switched off by mistake.

Work space and workstations

Where work is carried on in defined rooms (as opposed to the more familiar and transient 'care' related work), there must be adequate space to enable the work to be done safely. This will take into account the room area, height, any space taken up by furniture etc and the number of people working there. Although this is not likely to be a significant concern in most parts of care homes, it may apply in administration offices or workshops.

Any workstations provided (eg work surfaces and sinks in kitchen areas, ironing boards in laundries) must be suitable for the person using them and for the intended task. This may mean, for example, having equipment with adjustable height or providing standing platforms. People working out of doors must have somewhere to shelter from bad weather.

Seats should be provided where the work can be carried out sitting down.

Computer workstations are covered in Chapter 5, Work equipment.

STRUCTURAL CONSIDERATIONS

Entrances and exits

There must be safe ways into and out of workplaces. This may mean having to consider systems for ensuring that ice does not make outside routes dangerous in winter, dealing with difficult or awkward stairs and so on. The safety of these entrances and exits is also relevant to the safety of residents. Appropriate separation of pedestrians and vehicles may also be needed. You may have to restrict access to certain areas to authorised persons, and ensure that residents cannot get into areas such as cellars or lofts (which are generally difficult to negotiate). Where stairs or steps are unavoidable, there should be suitable handrails on at least one side, if not both. A lower rail may also be necessary to prevent people falling through any gaps between the stairs and the upper rail.

Given that many accidents are the result of slips, trips and falls on the same level, ensuring that spillages are cleaned up immediately, that regular maintenance prevents lifted carpet edges, holes or other damage occurring in floor surfaces, and that changes in floor levels are clearly and appropriately marked will significantly help to reduce these problems. Special lighting for external entrances and exits, especially if steps are involved, should also be considered. Your risk assessment should have identified and dealt with these aspects.

Floors

The condition of floors and other walking surfaces is a very important health and safety consideration and you have a duty to ensure that floors in your home do not pose any risk to health and safety. You should make sure that there are no holes, that floors are not unnecessarily uneven or slippery, and that suitable precautions are taken to prevent people falling (eg over loose mats) or otherwise harming themselves. This may mean taking steps to prevent people walking there (such as providing warning signs where floors are slippery (eg in kitchens), putting up barriers to restrict access where floors are damaged or uneven), or providing handrails to assist in the negotiation of slopes. Where the floor is likely to become wet, adequate drainage must be provided, and care should be taken to ensure that floors are kept free from obstructions likely to cause people to slip, trip or fall.

Again, flooring and associated safety measures must be of a high standard for the safety of residents.

Windows

Windows must be able to be opened (or closed) safely – they must not pose a risk to the person trying to open (or close) the window, either by falling out or causing an injury from straining to reach up or over any distances. They must also be safe when they are open: they should not open out directly onto any access or other route where they might be walked into. In addition, you must ensure that all the windows in your home can be cleaned safely; this may be achieved either through their design or construction, or by using devices such as anchorage points in the internal walls.

Windows and the glazed parts of any doors or walls must be made of a safety material or protected from breakage where necessary for reasons of health and safety (eg where staff and especially residents might walk into or fall against them). They must also be marked in some way so as to make them conspicuous.

Doors and gates should be fitted with appropriate safety devices: these depend on the type of door. For example:

- sliding doors should not be able to come off their tracks;
- up and over doors should be prevented from falling back;
- powered doors should have devices to prevent someone being injured by being trapped, as well as having a means of operation in the event of a power failure;
- doors capable of opening in both directions (such as are found between many kitchen and servery areas) should have a viewing panel so that users – including, if applicable, people in wheelchairs – can see through to the other side.

HOUSEKEEPING ARRANGEMENTS

Maintenance

The home and any equipment provided to comply with any of the legal requirements must be maintained in an efficient state, in efficient working order and in good repair. Your management system should provide for planned preventive maintenance procedures so that all equipment is regularly checked so as to minimise the risks of anything going wrong.

The term 'maintenance' includes appropriate cleaning. Maintenance of electrical systems is discussed in more detail in Chapter 10.

Your maintenance systems should also deal with the cleaning and treatment of hot water and/or air conditioning systems in order to prevent colonisation with the *Legionella* bacteria and possible outbreaks of Legionnaires' disease. Further information on this is provided in Chapters 6 and 10.

Cleaning and refuse disposal

The workplace, furniture, furnishings and fittings must be kept clean, and floors, walls and ceilings must be capable of being kept clean. The process of cleaning must not itself create a risk to health and safety; for example, wet floors may be slippery and care must be taken to ensure they cannot be walked on or that sufficient warnings are displayed. Boiler rooms should *not* be used for storage.

Refuse must be collected in suitable containers and not be allowed to accumulate in the workplace. Refuse from care homes may contain materials soiled with human excretions, and care must be taken to ensure that such waste is handled and disposed of correctly. The health aspects of clinical waste are discussed in Chapter 6, Hazardous substances.

WELFARE FACILITIES

Toilets

The toilet facilities must be sufficient for the numbers of staff and be readily accessible. The toilet areas must be well ventilated and lit, kept clean and in good condition and where necessary be separate for male and female employees, except where the toilets are in individual areas that are capable of being locked from the inside. The guidance recommends one toilet for 1 to 5 staff; two toilets for 6 to 25 staff; three toilets for 26 to 50 staff; four toilets for 51 to 75 staff and five toilets for 76 to 100 staff. One extra toilet should be provided for every 25 or fraction of 25 staff over 100. Where male staff are employed, the provision of urinals may be taken into account. Ideally, staff facilities should be separate from the residents' facilities. Under food safety legislation, separate designated toilet facilities should be provided for catering staff.

In addition, the toilets must be supplied with toilet paper and a coat hook; where females are employed, a means of disposing of soiled sanitary dressings is required.

Washing facilities

Sufficient washing facilities, including (where necessary for reasons of health and safety) showers, must also be provided. The ratios of washing facilities to staff are the same as those given above for toilets. Again, there must be sufficient facilities for the number of staff likely to use them. You must also allow for other special considerations: for example, the requirements under the food safety legislation; facilities in dirty areas (such as the laundry or sluice areas where soiled materials may be handled); and in the vicinity of toilets.

Each washing facility must be supplied with hot and cold (or warm) running water; soap, or other means of cleaning (additional items in the recognised 'dirty' areas may also be necessary); towels or other means of drying; be well ventilated and lit; and kept in an orderly manner. Separate facilities for male and female staff should be provided unless the facilities are in individual areas capable of being locked from the inside.

Changing areas and accommodation for clothing

Where special clothing has to be worn at work, adequate changing facilities must be provided; separate facilities for men and women may be necessary. Ideally, these should be next to the accommodation provided for clothing that is not being worn, and some washing facilities.

Accommodation must be provided for clothing not worn at work, or for special clothing left at work. This must be secure, and must include a means of drying and prevent contamination from soiled clothing to other clothing. Where clothing is likely to become soiled, special collection, storage and handling procedures may be necessary.

Rest and meal facilities

Readily accessible rest facilities must be provided: these must include facilities suitable for eating meals if meals are usually eaten at the workplace, or if there is a risk of food becoming contaminated by the work. The rest areas must include a means of protecting non-smokers from the effects of tobacco smoke either by segregation or by extraction systems, and should include areas suitable for pregnant women or nursing mothers to rest. In some cases (eg offices) it is sufficient for the workplace to be used as the rest area provided steps are taken to ensure that staff who are resting are not unduly disturbed by any work continuing around them.

Drinking water

An adequate supply of wholesome drinking water must be provided; ideally, this should be a mains supply, but container water is acceptable provided it is protected from contamination. A supply of cups must also be provided unless the drinking water is in the form of a water jet. The supply of drinking water must be clearly labelled as such, and supplies likely to be grossly contaminated must also be labelled to prevent anyone drinking unwholesome water inadvertently.

KEY POINTS

- Although care homes provide a domestic environment for the residents, they are also workplaces and therefore must comply with certain legal requirements.

- The legal requirements are contained in section 2(2) of HASAWA and in the Workplace (Health, Safety and Welfare) Regulations 1992.

- In practice the standards that ensure the health and comfort of the residents will probably be sufficient to ensure a suitable work environment for the staff, but extra consideration should be given to non-residential areas such as kitchens, maintenance workshops and external workplaces such as gardeners' sheds.

- The various aspects of the workplace that must be considered include:
  - temperature, ventilation, lighting;
  - maintenance, cleaning and refuse disposal;

– welfare facilities such as toilets, washing facilities, changing facilities, accommodation for clothing, provision of drinking water and rest areas;

– structural considerations such as windows, doors, walls, ceilings, floors, traffic routes, and entrances and exits.

Relevant guidance

L24 *Workplace health, safety and welfare: ACOP*

HS(G)132 *How to deal with sick building syndrome – guidance for employers, building owners and building managers*

HS(G)155 *Slips and trips*

Safe disposal of clinical waste

IND(G)170L *Workplace health, safety and welfare* (free)

All the above are available from HSE Books (see p 176).

5 Work equipment

Care homes are likely to use a wide range of equipment, from mechanical hoists for lifting and moving residents, through display screen equipment (DSE, VDUs) to various items of machinery used in food preparation, as well as lawn mowers and strimmers used in grounds maintenance.

Section 2(2) of HASAWA requires all plant (which includes equipment, machinery and appliances) provided for use at work to be safe and without risk to health. This general requirement under the duty to ensure the health and safety of employees is supported by the Provision and Use of Work Equipment Regulations 1992, which apply to all work equipment (but there is a transitional period in effect until 1 January 1997 before they come fully into operation).

Section 6 of HASAWA places certain duties related to health and safety on manufacturers and suppliers of articles intended for use at work. In addition, there are some pre-1974 Regulations that apply to certain dangerous machines; some of these Regulations may be relevant to the machinery used in your kitchens and/or laundry. This chapter discusses the main requirements relating to work equipment.

DEFINITION

'Work equipment' is defined as machinery, appliances, apparatus or tools, or an assembly of components that function together as a unit used at work. In care homes this will include vacuum cleaners, catering and laundry equipment, maintenance tools, gardening equipment, hoists and (possibly) resuscitation equipment.

'Use' is given a wide definition, and includes starting, stopping, programming, setting, transporting, repairing, modifying, maintaining, servicing and cleaning. This means that your risk assessments must take into account all the risks associated with all these factors, not just the operation.

SUITABILITY

Design

Designers, manufacturers and suppliers must ensure that work equipment is designed so as to be safe and without risks to health when used for its intended purpose and in foreseeable conditions of use.

The broad definition of 'use' includes the setting of machinery, as well as its actual operation, cleaning and maintenance. In addition, relevant health and safety related information about the safe operation of the equipment must be provided by the supplier or manufacturer or designer. When the information is revised for any reason, the updated information must also be provided. Retailers do not have the same duty to provide information but many can and will do so if they are told that the equipment is for use at work. If the retailer cannot provide the information, you should contact the manufacturer or supplier direct.

Manufacturers' instructions are a very important source of information and will explain safe operating practices and any limitations of the equipment.

Installers must also ensure that any equipment that is installed is safe and without risks to health in relation to the installation.

Intended use

Designers and manufacturers can only indicate the foreseeable safe methods and conditions of use, so it is up to you to ensure that any equipment you purchase or hire is suitable for the intended task(s) and conditions of use. For example, many establishments use domestic refrigerators or microwave ovens that are generally unsuitable for heavy usage and therefore do not reach safe operating temperatures or break down regularly.

Industrial units are designed for the greater volume of work and higher performance standards and are a more economical and safer option. Likewise, electrical equipment intended for external use, or for use in wet conditions, should be designed and chosen for those conditions, because they will incorporate relevant safety features that are not always found on ordinary appliances.

Before you purchase or hire any equipment think about what you want it to do, who is going to use it, how it is going to be used and under what conditions. Consulting your staff who will have to use it will provide a lot of valuable information on problems that you might not be aware of. You also need to consider whether the equipment is going to pose additional risks to people working nearby, as well as any risks posed by the equipment itself.

The purchase of second-hand work equipment should be avoided.

SPECIFIC HAZARDS

Besides the dangers created by the actual power source of the equipment (eg electricity: see also Chapter 10), you must also be aware of the likely hazards associated with work equipment in your home. These hazards may arise from:

- contact with moving parts;
- becoming entangled or entrapped with parts of the machinery – loose clothing and long, loose hair are often caught up;
- being struck by a moving part;
- being hit by an item that has been ejected, either because a component breaks up or because a part works loose.

In many cases the work equipment found in care homes is more likely to be a hazard because of its power source (eg electricity) than through any dangerous parts, but you must consider that it is likely that inherently dangerous equipment may be present in your kitchens, laundry and maintenance workshops.

SAFE WORKING PRACTICES

Training, information and instructions

You have a duty under section 2(2) of HASAWA to provide sufficient information, instruction and training to enable staff to work safely and without risk to their health. This is dealt with in detail by the Provision and Use of Work Equipment Regulations 1992: they specifically require adequate health and safety information and written instructions to be given to staff and to any supervisors or managers of staff using the equipment. The information and instructions must deal with the conditions and method of using the equipment, any foreseeable abnormal or emergency situations and the necessary actions, and any other information gained from past experience with the equipment.

The information and instructions must be comprehensible. This means that you may have to consider foreign language translations if English is not the first language of some of your staff and take into account any disabilities of your staff (eg provide literature in braille for visually impaired people). The Health and Safety Executive are now producing an increasing range of foreign language health and safety-related information.

Similar provisions require people using the equipment, and their supervisors and managers, to be trained in its proper use; this will include following manufacturers' instructions, any limitations, emergency actions and the risks associated with the equipment and the control measures that are necessary.

Authorised use

In some cases you may need to restrict the use of certain work equipment to named individuals – people who have received adequate training or experience and who are competent to use, or supervise the use of, the equipment. There are also special legal controls (discussed under 'Dangerous machinery', below) that restrict some activities.

During maintenance work, you may have to prevent the operation of certain equipment until it has been officially released for use: equipment is 'locked off' in order to prevent accidental use. An example of this would be the cleaning of the 'dumb waiter' (a small lift that transports food from the kitchen to the dining room): this must be deliberately put out of operation so that the person cleaning it does not become trapped because someone tries to use it from the other end.

Controls

All work equipment should have controls so that the operator can affect the status of the equipment. In many cases the controls will be simple 'on–off' switches so that the equipment can be safely turned off if there are any problems. There are additional safety features associated with electrical appliances (eg fuses). With more complex equipment there may be a 'hierarchy' of controls; for example, start and/or operating speed controls, ordinary stop controls, and emergency stop controls that override all preceding controls and bring the equipment to a safe halt.

Preventive and protective measures

As with all control measures the most effective method of control is to remove or eliminate the hazard at source – for example, by careful design and selection of equipment. If the hazard cannot be removed, guards may be needed to prevent contact with any moving parts; manufacturers will provide any necessary guards. It may be possible to position the equipment so that it does not represent a danger to anyone who is operating it or is nearby. It is often possible to have interlocking guards so that the equipment cannot be operated unless the guard is in position. Risks can also be reduced by restricting the people authorised to operate the equipment. Personal protective equipment should be provided only as a last resort.

When specific precautionary measures are needed for the equipment to be operated safely, staff should be trained in their use and understand what dangers the control measures are meant to deal with. You may need to back up these control measures with formal disciplinary procedures for staff who disregard the instructions. Again, staff must be aware of the consequences of not following instructions.

DANGEROUS MACHINERY

The Offices, Shops and Railway Premises Act 1963 and the Prescribed Dangerous Machines Order 1964 prevent anyone operating any of the listed dangerous machines unless they have been given full instructions and training for operating the machine, the associated dangers and any necessary precautions, or they are supervised by a person competent to operate the machine. The machines to which these restrictions apply include:

Power driven

- worm-type mincing machines;
- rotary knife bowl-type chopping machines;
- dough brakes and dough mixers;
- food mixing machines when used with attachments for mincing, slicing, chipping or any other cutting operation, or for crumbling;
- pie and tart making machines;
- vegetable slicing machines;
- wrapping and packing machines;
- garment presses;
- various saws.

Not necessarily driven by mechanical power

- circular knife slicing machines used for cutting foods;
- potato chipping machines;
- guillotines.

Although the wide-ranging legal controls affecting 'factories' do not apply to care homes, there is a very similar set of Regulations under the Factories Act 1961 which lists virtually identical dangerous equipment, with the addition of the following laundry equipment: hydro-extractors; calenders and washing machines. You may therefore have to consider appropriate procedures and controls for their operation.

NOISE

Although care homes are probably not noisy workplaces as such, some activities call for associated noise levels to be dealt with. One example is gardening equipment (eg strimmers), especially if it is used for long periods.

The Noise at Work Regulations 1989 define three action levels for noise:

- 85dB: this is the first action level;
- 90dB: this is the second action level;
- 200 pascals: this is the third (peak) action level.

The first and second action levels relate to daily exposures and take into account noise variations during the day. The third action level applies only to short explosive sounds, such as gunshots.

Ordinary speech is around 65dB; noise levels of up to 60dB are not reckoned to affect the ability of people to work normally. If the noise levels reach 85dB or the peak action level, however, an assessment of the noise exposure must be carried out. As a general rule, if you have to shout to be heard over two metres away, an assessment is probably necessary. If the noise level is at least 85dB, ear protectors must be provided if requested. If the noise exposure reaches 90dB, ear protectors must be provided in any event – and employees have a legal duty to wear them – and the area must be marked as an ear protection zone. Records of any such assessments should be kept, and reviewed and revised as necessary.

Personal protective equipment such as ear protectors should be used as a last resort where the noise level cannot be reduced sufficiently by other means.

DISPLAY SCREEN EQUIPMENT

Display screen equipment (DSE), or more familiarly visual display units (VDUs), are discussed here although they are subject to their own specific rules.

The Health and Safety (Display Screen Equipment) Regulations 1992 contain special rules about the use of display screen equipment. It is unlikely that these Regulations will be of major significance to care homes but they may apply where people are dedicated to office/administration work involving regular use of VDUs.

The Regulations apply to any alpha-numeric or graphic display screens (ie screens that display text, numbers or pictures); this includes VDUs and microfiche screens. Portable systems used for short periods, calculators, window typewriters and cash registers are not covered by the Regulations, but any risks they may pose (such as poor operating posture) would have to be included in the general risk assessment and would be covered by the 'Work equipment' Regulations.

All DSE workstations must be examined to assess the risks associated with the work. If any risks are identified, they must be reduced to the lowest level reasonably practicable. The assessments should be reviewed regularly and revised as necessary. The term 'workstation' includes not only the actual screen but also the desk, chair, other equipment associated with the screen (eg modems, printers), the surrounding work environment, and even the suitability of the software. The Regulations and accompanying guidance set down the minimum standards for workstations (the main aspects are discussed below). Equipment in use before 1993 will not be affected by these workstation rules until the end of 1996.

In practice, it is important that the chair is fully adjustable so that the user can work at the correct height to prevent arm/wrist strains, and so that there is full and proper back support. There should be enough space on the desk for the user to work comfortably and with the keyboard positioned correctly; document-holders and foot-rests may need to be provided. The screen height should be adjustable so that the screen is at eye level to prevent the user having to look up or down. Lighting is another important factor and screens should be positioned so as to minimise glare from any light sources; extra lights may be required for reading the input data, and these should not interfere with the screen. Excessive noise (especially from dot matrix printers) or heat must also be dealt with. Software should be suitable for the standard of the user; where possible, it should not dictate the speed of work.

The Regulations also provide for regular breaks away from the screen work. The official guidance recommends a break of five to ten minutes for every hour of use. This does not necessarily mean coffee breaks, but rather doing non-screen work such as filing or photocopying so as to give the eyes and hand/arm muscles a rest. The breaks should be left to the discretion of the users where possible but it is the employer's responsibility to ensure that they *are* taken. The accumulation of breaks to provide a shorter day should be prohibited.

Finally, employers must also offer eyesight tests to designated users who request them, at regular intervals thereafter, and whenever visual difficulties are experienced with screen work. If glasses or other corrective appliances are needed, the employer has to pay for them but only to the extent that they are necessary for the screen work – where multi-focal lenses are required by the user, the employer has to pay only for the costs related to the screen work.

Staff should receive information, instruction and training in relation to display screen work and workstations, the hazards, risks and any necessary precautions; these will include the need to take breaks away from the screen and the right to have eyesight tests.

Employers have very similar duties to protect and advise 'operators' (ie self-employed people or agency staff) who use display screens for the employer's business.

KEY POINTS

- 'Work equipment' includes machinery, tools, appliances, apparatus or assembly of components operating as a single unit used at work.

- 'Use' is defined as starting, stopping, setting, programming, cleaning, repairing, modifying, transporting, servicing, maintaining and operating any work equipment.

- Work equipment must be suitable for its intended task and the intended conditions of use.

- Staff must be given adequate and understandable training, information and instruction on how to use the equipment, as well as on any emergency actions that may be needed, and any precautions necessary for health and safety.

- Designers, manufacturers and suppliers have a duty to ensure the safety of any equipment supplied for use at work, and to provide relevant health and safety information about that equipment.

- Some work equipment may require noise assessments to be undertaken and appropriate actions taken.

- The type of danger associated with any particular piece of equipment must be considered in the risk assessment (eg contact with moving parts, ejection, entrapment or entanglement).

- The control 'hierarchy' is to eliminate the hazard at source (by designing out the hazard etc), by guarding or safe positioning, by restricting use and – as a last resort – by providing personal protective equipment.

- There are special rules about the safety of display screen workstations and work practices. The workstations must meet minimum standards with regard to the display screen and related equipment (desks, chairs, lighting etc) and users must take regular breaks away from their screen work; they are also entitled to eyesight tests in relation to their screen work.

Relevant guidance

L22 *Work equipment – guidance on the Provision and Use of Work Equipment Regulations 1992*

L26 *Display screen equipment – guidance on Regulations*

Both the above are available from HSE Books (see p 176).

6 Hazardous substances

In the simplest terms, 'hazardous substances' may be considered as substances capable of causing adverse health effects, regardless of whether they are chemicals, biological agents such as bacteria, or gaseous fumes or vapours. Virtually all work involves some exposure to hazardous substances but the nature and degree of that exposure will depend on the type of undertaking. All such exposures are dealt with by the Control of Substances Hazardous to Health Regulations 1994 (COSHH).

Hazardous substances in care homes can include cleaning chemicals, cleaning agents used in (or dust generated by) maintenance work, fertiliser and pesticides used in the gardens, and biological agents from soiled linen or body fluids, and possibly from water systems contaminated with *Legionella* bacteria (see also Chapter 10). It is also worth noting that some apparently harmless foodstuffs can cause health problems such as allergies and dermatitis. The duty to ensure the health and safety of staff is owed to each individual member of staff, so the possibility of someone being susceptible to a particular substance must be taken into account.

This chapter looks at the main requirements of the COSHH Regulations, provides practical points on the safe use and handling of hazardous substances and sets out the correct procedures for dealing with clinical waste.

CONTROL OF SUBSTANCES HAZARDOUS TO HEALTH REGULATIONS 1994

These Regulations form the most significant advance in improving the standards of staff health at work, and follow the now familiar routine of identifying the hazards associated with the exposure to any substances that may create a health problem, and eliminating or at least adequately controlling them.

Definition

COSHH provides a detailed definition of 'substances that are hazardous to health' – a substance that is labelled as being:

- very toxic or toxic (skull and crossbones);
- harmful or irritant (St Andrew's cross);
- corrosive (two horizontal, dripping test tubes over a hand and bench).

All these labels are black symbols on an orange background and will be clearly visible on the container, where they are appropriate:

- any substance that has prescribed exposure limits;
- biological agents including micro-organisms or human endoparasites (parasitic worms) capable of causing infections, allergies, toxicity, or other human health hazards;
- substantial quantities of dust;
- any other substance capable of creating a health hazard similar to the substances listed above.

COSHH does not apply to the hazards created by asbestos, lead or ionising radiations; these are covered by their own Regulations. If your staff are likely to come into contact with any of these substances, specialist help should be sought.

Also excluded from COSHH are flammable and/or explosive substances that pose a threat to safety (causing injury) as opposed to health (causing illness), but if these types of substances are present in your workplace they should be included in the general risk assessment required by the 1992 'Management' Regulations.

Duties

You must assess the risks associated with the exposure to any hazardous substances in your home and decide on effective control measures. The assessment must be reviewed regularly and be revised as necessary if it becomes out of date. It is good practice to keep written details of the assessments made.

Once the hazardous exposures have been identified, you must take action to prevent the exposure or to control it adequately. Any control measures provided must be properly used, maintained in an efficient state, and returned to any accommodation provided for it. Defects/faults must be reported. Some engineering controls (eg local exhaust ventilation) must be examined and tested at the specified intervals; the associated records must be kept for five years. Even after control measures have been provided, you must continue to monitor exposure to any hazardous substances at work. This monitoring will ensure that such exposure is kept within safe limits and will also highlight any failures, which can then be dealt with immediately.

Although health surveillance is unlikely to be needed in the conditions specified under COSHH, it may be necessary in situations in which there is an obvious health problem (eg dermatitis) as contained in the 1992 'Management' Regulations. Any health records created for identifiable individuals are subject to the normal rules of confidentiality and must be kept for 40 years.

Finally, you must provide your staff with information, instruction and training to enable them to understand the risks associated with the exposure to the hazardous substance and the necessary precautions.

PRACTICES

Assessment

An effective way to begin your assessment of any exposures to hazardous substances is to make an inventory of all the substances that are or are likely to be used or handled in your home. For chemicals this is simply a matter of listing all the chemical agents on the premises – it does not matter at this stage whether they are hazardous or not – and making sure that there are safety data sheets for each one. As with work equipment (discussed in the previous chapter), manufacturers and suppliers must provide relevant health and safety information about their products (in the form of safety data sheets), and keep you updated with any significant developments or revisions.

Retailers do not have the same duties but will usually be able to provide the information if you tell them that the substances are for use at work. If the information is not available, it may be obtained directly from the manufacturer or supplier. The safety data sheets should be kept in a central file and copies given to the appropriate departments or staff for local reference.

Once the inventory is completed the substances can be checked to see if they are covered by COSHH. To start with, you should check the labels to see if they correspond to the ones mentioned above. Container labels provide much useful information, so it is important that, if decanting substances from large containers to smaller containers is carried out in your home, the corresponding information is provided on the new container. However, whenever possible, decanting should not be permitted because it places more responsibility on your management controls to ensure that all the relevant information is transferred each time and that suitable receiving containers are used. For example, some chemicals react together to form more noxious substances; sometimes the wrong containers will be used (eg lemonade bottles) and this could seriously mislead not only your staff but also your residents.

More detailed information will be contained in safety data sheets; this will include an indication of any hazards associated with the substance, the precautions to be taken, important storage and disposal information and any other relevant details such as appropriate first-aid measures and compatibility with other substances.

You will also need to consider what form the substance is likely to be in (ie solid, liquid or gaseous) because this will show the possible route of entry into the body. The routes of entry are by inhalation (breathing the substance in), by ingestion (eating or drinking the substance) or through skin absorption (either directly through the skin or through open cuts and lesions). Conditions such as dermatitis react with the natural substances in the skin, causing the outer skin layers to dry out and harden.

You will also have to find out who is exposed to the hazardous substances identified and how long exposure lasts.

Unfortunately, biological hazards are not conveniently labelled and you will have to look at each work activity to see if there is any associated health risk. Activities in which biological agents may be encountered include laundry and care work, especially with very infirm residents; in both these situations there is a risk of contact with soiled linen or other articles; contact with any body fluids also poses a risk. (Blood-borne infections are dealt with in Chapter 11.) *Legionella* bacteria colonising poorly maintained water systems are also covered by COSHH(more information is given in Chapter 10). A pond or other water in the grounds that requires maintenance are recognised sources of infection (such as leptospirosis, also called Weil's disease) from water contaminated by rats' urine.

Similarly, some apparently harmless substances and hazardous products produced as a result of a work activity (eg dust generated by woodworking, for which an occupational exposure limit has been laid down) must be assessed because there may not be any readily available information, nor even indications of there being any associated health risks.

It is essential that you consider not only the risks posed by the hazardous substances but also how they are actually used. Some chemicals, when mixed together, react to form a more hazardous substance: for example, some toilet cleaners and bleach react and release a toxic gas. Make sure that staff do not use stronger concentrations of the substances in the mistaken belief that this will be more effective. Considerable effort is put into finding the most effective concentration at which a chemical will work – increasing the recommended concentration in use will not always improve performance but may well increase the associated health risks.

Accidental exposures such as dealing with spillages and leakages must also be taken into consideration.

Controls

As with any other control measures, there is a preferred order for dealing with a hazardous substance:

- eliminate the hazard at source;
- use a less hazardous substance instead;
- provide appropriate engineering controls (eg vents and air extractors) so as to reduce:
  - the number of people exposed,
  - the duration of exposure;
- provide personal protective equipment (PPE) – but only as a last resort.

It is unlikely in care homes that sophisticated engineering controls will be necessary and the control measure options are more likely to rely on proper information, instruction and training, safe systems of work and the provision of PPE. This does not mean that other controls may be automatically discounted; you must decide on the most appropriate measures for your own situation.

The safe systems of work should not only indicate the correct procedures to be followed, but should also include active monitoring strategies so that staff are encouraged to pay attention to their own health and report any signs of problems. An early investigation can then be carried out before a problem becomes significant.

CLINICAL WASTE

It is quite likely that some work activities in care homes will involve dealing with body fluids and excretions. It is important that such work be carried out in accordance with accepted standards of good practice, not only for the safety of the staff but also of anyone else who has to handle the waste subsequently. Clinical wastes are covered by COSHH.

Classification

There are five recognised classes of clinical waste:

Class A: human tissues and/or blood (whether infected or not).

Class B: contaminated disposable 'sharps' such as used hypodermic needles, cartridges and broken glass.

Class C: microbiological cultures from research laboratories etc.

Class D: certain pharmaceutical products and chemical wastes (eg out-of-date drugs).

Class E: disposable containers for urine, faeces and other bodily secretions and excretions that are not covered by Class A (eg disposable bedpans and/or liners, incontinence pads, stoma bags and urine containers).

Class E and, to a lesser extent, Classes A and B will be most relevant to care homes. Although the level of risk associated with items in Class E is likely to be fairly low, it is impossible to assess exactly what the risk is, so it is important that all such items are treated as clinical waste. The offensive nature of items in this class must also be taken into consideration.

Storage

Clinical waste

A clinical waste storage area should be:

- designated solely for that purpose;
- secure against all unauthorised entry whether human or animal;
- enclosed;
- well drained, ventilated and lit;
- readily accessible.

It should also be sited well away from food and public routes, and not be offensive to adjacent areas.

Regular collections should be arranged so that clinical waste is not allowed to accumulate.

Your procedures for storing clinical waste should include dealing with spillages (ie containment and decontamination measures).

Sharps

Where Class B waste is generated (ie contaminated sharps), special sharps containers that meet the appropriate British Standard (BS 7320), or the European equivalent, must be provided and used. In no circumstances should other household containers be used instead, because sharps pose considerable risks to subsequent handlers. Never fill a sharps container more than three-quarters full, and always ensure it is sealed shut. Sharps containers should never be placed in bags for disposal. Security at sharps storage areas may need to be tighter than for other clinical wastes, especially to prevent used needles being stolen – this is particularly relevant where collections are irregular or more than a week apart.

Disposal

Clinical waste should be collected into colour coded, disposable plastic sacks which must meet the appropriate British Standard (BS 6642) or the European equivalent. As with sharps containers, the sacks should never be filled more than three-quarters full and should be securely tied round the neck. The colour coding is:

Class A and B wastes	yellow	incineration only
Class E wastes	yellow with black stripe	suitable for landfill
Normal household waste	black	domestic collection

It is your responsibility to ensure that the wastes are disposed of safely and properly. The domestic waste collection service is not a proper method of disposal. There are several options for ensuring correct and proper disposal, which may involve the local authority clinical waste disposal service or private contractors. Under environmental protection law you are responsible for the waste from 'cradle to grave' – from the time the waste is produced until it is safely disposed of – and all the necessary certificates and contracts should be kept as evidence of sound disposal methods.

Advice on local facilities and services may be obtained from the local waste regulation authorities.

Training

Your staff should be trained in all aspects of dealing with clinical waste, including accidents or spillages. In particular, the training should deal with the associated risks, and necessary precautions such as good standards of personal hygiene, use of personal protective equipment and reporting of any incidents that could lead to infection.

Records should be kept of all training given to staff and refresher training organised as needed from time to time.

- The Control of Substances Hazardous to Health Regulations 1994 (COSHH) set out the main legal controls over occupational health risks.

- COSHH requires assessments to be made of all exposures to hazardous substances in the workplace and their subsequent elimination or adequate control.

- Hazardous substances or substances hazardous to health include chemicals labelled as toxic or very toxic, irritant, harmful or corrosive; biological agents likely to cause infections or allergies etc; large amounts of dusts and any other substances likely to have an adverse effect on health.

- Hazardous substances in care homes include cleaning chemicals and cleaning agents used in maintenance work; fertilisers and pesticides used in garden maintenance; and clinical wastes, especially bodily fluids, secretions and excretions.

Relevant guidance

L5 *General COSHH, carcinogens and biological agents: ACOP*

HS(G)97 *A step by step guide to COSHH assessment*

HS(G)110 *Seven steps to successful substitution of hazardous substances*

EH40 *Occupational exposure limits* (revised annually)

Health surveillance under COSHH: a guide for employers

Safe disposal of clinical waste

IND(G)84 *Leptospirosis* (free)

IND(G)136L *COSHH: a brief guide for employers* (free)

All the above are available from HSE Books (see p 176).

7 Manual handling

As discussed in Chapter 3, manual handling activities account for the greatest number of work-related accidents, and musculo-skeletal injuries are the most common job-related injuries reported. There is an obvious link.

In care homes, manual handling is likely to be particularly significant, especially where the residents are unable to move around or act independently. Whilst lifting and carrying residents may be the area for greatest consideration, do not forget that manual handling also occurs in virtually every other job. Heavy loads that have to be moved will almost certainly exist in the kitchen, laundry, maintenance, gardening and office departments, as well as in the direct care of residents.

This chapter summarises the main legal rules and looks in more detail at some of the factors you must consider when managing manual handling in your home.

MANUAL HANDLING OPERATIONS REGULATIONS 1992

Under these Regulations, manual handling activities are defined as 'the transporting or supporting of a load by hand or other bodily force, including the lifting, lowering, pushing, pulling, carrying or moving of a load'.

The Regulations are very simple and basically require you to avoid all manual handling activities where it is reasonably practicable to do so. If you cannot avoid such activities you must assess every manual handling activity where there is a risk of injury and reduce those risks to the lowest level reasonably practicable. Again, your assessments must be reviewed regularly and revised as necessary.

You must also tell people who carry out manual handling activities the weight of the loads they have to lift and the heaviest side of any asymmetrical (unbalanced) loads – these may be indicated on the load or its packaging.

Staff must make full and proper use of anything provided by the employer in compliance with these Regulations. They also have a legal duty to notify the employer of any health condition that might make them more susceptible to injury.

PRACTICES

The 1992 Regulations mean that you must consider every work activity that involves manual handling and decide whether you can eliminate the need for that activity. For example, can goods be delivered direct to the storage area rather than to an intermediate place, or can the work area layout be redesigned to eliminate the need for manual handling? Alternatively, some mechanical aid or aids (eg a hoist) may remove (or at least reduce) the need for manual handling activities.

It is worth noting that injuries and ill-health associated with manual handling tend to build up over time and are less often caused by a single event.

Assessments

Where it is not reasonably practicable to eliminate the need for manual handling activities, you must assess the risks of injury associated with each of these activities. In doing the assessment you must take into account the load, the task, the place where the work will be done and the individual abilities of the people doing the work.

The load

Loads are divided into two types: animate (eg residents) and inanimate (eg boxes, furniture). Although the principles of manual handling are the same in both cases, the execution is very different.

Regardless of the type of load, the following factors should be considered in all manual handling activities:

- weight of the load;
- size (bulky or unwieldy);
- stability (rigidness or floppiness);
- ability to hold the load securely (eg convenient hand holds; or physical characteristics that make it difficult to hold, eg sharp edges).

There are no defined numerical weights for lifting residents. The emphasis must be on avoiding, as much as possible, any manual handling activities that involve residents. (The Royal College of Nursing has withdrawn its guidance on reasonable weights for one person and two people lifting a patient but has a code of practice and guidance on patient handling; see p 80). Numerical weight limits for static loads are given in HSE's guidance booklet L23 (see p 80).

The position of the load in relation to the person(s) performing the manual handling activity will significantly affect their ability to lift. The closer the load is to the centre of the body of the person performing the lift, the less the risk of injury and the more efficient, comfortable and safe the operation is.

Depending on the type of home, there may be other factors that need to be considered, such as associated medical equipment (eg gas cylinders, intravenous drips). The residents' ability to help themselves will also influence the degree of risk attached to manual handling work. You will need to consider how the resident may react. Will they be passive or react violently? Are they likely to have a spasm or fit and suddenly go rigid or floppy? Are they able to move themselves to a limited extent, needing only occasional support? Each resident's personal care plan can be used as the basis of a manual handling assessment: it will provide details about the 'load' (the resident), procedures to be followed, equipment to be used and so on.

If the residents are frail or elderly (or both), errors in the manual handling technique may cause pain and further suffering. The dignity of the residents should also be taken into account.

The task

Several factors must be considered when assessing manual handling work. You will need to decide how the load is held in relation to the body of the person doing the work. Are any awkward or difficult body movements required, such as bending, twisting or stooping? Poor posture caused by having to reach up, for example to get books from a high shelf, will also lead to problems.

The distance the load has to be moved is another important factor, and may involve repetitive movements from a high position to a low one, or long walking distances between rooms. When long distances have to be travelled it is good practice to plan your route and ensure it is clear and unobstructed before you set out. It will certainly be helpful to know before commencing the activity whether there are changes in floor level and, if so, exactly where they are.

The frequency of the task should also be considered because repeated and prolonged manual handling duties will cause 'creeping fatigue', which gradually reduces the ability of an individual to work efficiently and safely. When prolonged and/or frequent manual handling work has to be done, rest or recovery periods may be needed. Likewise, holding fixed postures for any length of time, perhaps in supporting a resident during walking exercise, will cause problems.

When personal protective equipment (PPE) has to be used, its effect on the activity should be considered.

Whilst manual handling tasks should be assessed individually in relation to the person actually doing them, it will be useful to build up 'generic' (or 'type') assessments for similar tasks so that an initial outline can be developed as a basis for all the more specific assessments. If generic assessments are used, it is important for all the specific differences to be thought out in order to achieve a representative assessment.

The working environment

Once you have considered the load and the task, you need to look at the physical conditions in which the work is being done. These will include:

- Restrictions on space (eg is posture adversely affected by limited space?).
- Consideration of any uneven or slippery floors or changes in floor level.
- Temperature and humidity (eg in many kitchens, laundries and bathrooms).
- Lighting.

One indirect problem is how to provide enough storage facilities to eliminate the need for the intermediate transfer of loads. Another comes from poorly designed facilities which prevent the correct posture being adopted.

The individual

When all the other factors have been considered, the capabilities of the people doing the work must be considered. This is probably the most important factor and the one over which you will have least influence in terms of adaptation. Remember that you always fit a job to a person – never a person to a job.

Your other assessments on the load, task and working environment will tell you whether the work will require any special physical attributes (eg considerable strength or a particular height). You will also have to decide whether the task poses an unacceptable risk to pregnant women or people with specific health problems (eg bad back, hernia). Pre-employment health questionnaires and interviews may avoid some problems. Some tasks may call for specialist knowledge and/or training.

Finally, you need to remember that individuals do not remain the same and there will be some variation in a person's capabilities as they grow older or as certain physiological conditions develop. For example, a pregnant woman will probably be able to lift or move loads quite normally in the initial stages of pregnancy but, as the baby grows, so the woman may become more tired and will find it more difficult to hold loads closely and securely.

The type of clothing worn by staff doing manual handling work is very important and should allow enough movement to be able to get into all the proper positions for the task in hand. Trousers and flat shoes are probably sensible choices.

CONTROL AND REDUCTION MEASURES

When your assessments have identified all the associated hazards, you set about eliminating or controlling them. Obvious controls are the use of height-adjustable beds and hoists to move residents who are immobile. Other aids for moving residents include turntables on which a resident can stand to be turned round to face in another direction. Turning-sheets may ease the effort involved in turning residents in bed; these allow a low-friction sheet to be placed under the resident, so that it can be easily pulled to move the resident to a different position. Various slings and belts exist to assist in manually handling people.

Inanimate loads may be divided into smaller units, and trolleys provided to reduce the effort of transferring goods.

When effective control measures can be put in place without excessive cost (eg by simply redesigning the work area), this would certainly be considered to be 'reasonably practicable'.

Other control measures include rotating manual handling work so as to avoid unnecessary strains on one person from prolonged, repetitive and otherwise poor postures and the like. Many organisations now appoint 'manual handling' or 'back care' advisers in each of their departments: it is their duty to co-ordinate all manual handling matters and, more importantly, to keep a watch on the practices adopted during the course of the work and to offer on-the-job support to staff, especially new members.

Training is another important control measure and it is vitally important that all staff receive training appropriate to their work duties and their responsibilities.

KEY POINTS

- Manual handling work is the main cause of occupational accidents.
- The effects of poor manual handling techniques tend to build up over time, and are less often attributable to any single event.

- Manual handling work should be avoided where reasonably practicable; if this is not possible, the risks of injury must be assessed and appropriate control measures implemented.

- Any manual handling assessments carried out should deal with the load, the task, the working environment and the individual capabilities of the person(s) performing the task.

- The personal care plan should form the basis of an assessment of manual handling of each resident, and of subsequent records.

- Control measures include the provision of suitable mechanical and other aids (eg resident hoists, stairlifts); the redesign of work areas and systems; and training programmes.

Relevant guidance

L23 *Manual handling: guidance on the Manual Handling Operations Regulations 1992*

HS(G)115 *Manual handling – solutions you can handle*

HS(G)137 *Health risk management – a practical guide for managers in small and medium sized enterprises*

Getting to grips with handling problems – worked examples of assessment and reduction of risk in the Health Service

Guidance on manual handling of loads in the Health Service

IND(G)109 *Lighten the load – guidance for employers on musculoskeletal disorders*

IND(G)110 *Lighten the load – guidance for employees on musculoskeletal disorders*

All the above are available from HSE Books (see p 176).

Royal College of Nursing Code of Practice for patient handling (1996)

Introducing a safer patient handling policy (1996)

Manual handling assessment in hospitals and the community

These are available from the Royal College of Nursing (see p 177).

8 First aid

First aid is the initial medical treatment given after an injury has been received. It may save lives and, if applied correctly, almost certainly assists and improves recovery. There are right and wrong procedures in first aid treatments and it is obviously important that the person administering the treatment is properly trained.

With regard to work, the Health and Safety (First Aid) Regulations 1981 require employers to provide adequate and appropriate first aid resources; these include first aid equipment and facilities and suitably trained staff. Although the Regulations are designed to protect staff only, you must remember that the residents may occasionally require first aid.

This chapter looks at the rules in the 'First Aid' Regulations, and discusses what constitutes 'adequate and appropriate' first aid provisions.

FIRST AID ARRANGEMENTS

Staff must be told about all the first aid arrangements in the home; this will include the names and means of contacting the trained first aiders (or appointed person(s)), the location of first aid boxes and any first aid room. The information given must be understandable, so you must make special efforts to help staff whose first language is not English. This information should be given to staff at the start of their employment; if there are any changes, these should be explained to existing staff as well.

When contractors are working on the premises, there may be a written agreement for them to use the first aid arrangements at the home; staff from the home and from the contractors must be told about these arrangements.

FIRST AID EQUIPMENT AND FACILITIES

'First aid equipment and facilities' includes first aid boxes, first aid kits and first aid rooms, any combination of which may be necessary to provide adequate first aid.

The first aid resources provided by the employer should take into account:

- number of staff;
- nature of the business;
- nature and degree of risk;
- size and layout of the workplace;
- availability of local accident and emergency facilities.

It is likely that care homes will employ a relatively small number of staff, in a compact location (ie one building) and, with the exception of a few known hazardous areas (such as kitchens and maintenance workshops), will be fairly low risk. This is a generalisation and your own circumstances must be taken into account when deciding what is adequate for your home.

First aid boxes and first aid kits

All first aid boxes must be readily accessible and readily identifiable (a white cross on a green background). Most suppliers provide a range of sizes depending on the number of staff. The boxes will include the following basic items:

- guidance card
- individually wrapped sterile adhesive dressings (kitchens may require coloured plasters for easy detection)
- sterile eye pads with attachments
- individually wrapped triangular bandages

- safety pins
- medium-sized, individually wrapped, sterile, unmedicated, wound dressings – 10cm × 8cm
- large, individually wrapped, sterile, unmedicated, wound dressings – 13cm × 9cm
- extra-large, individually wrapped, sterile, unmedicated, wound dressings – 28cm × 17.5cm

Where mains water is not readily available, 900ml of sterile water or sterile normal saline solution (0.9 per cent) in three 300ml containers should be provided for eye irrigation.

Water, soap and a means of drying should also be readily available.

It may be necessary to provide extra items for specific hazards (eg burn sprays for use in kitchens). Many organisations also provide disposable airway tubes to prevent direct contact with a victim's mouth during mouth-to-mouth resuscitation and disposable gloves to prevent contact with blood or other body fluids.

Medicines, including headache pills, must never be kept in a first aid box because first aiders are not medically qualified to dispense them. There is nothing to prevent self-service dispensing units being provided so that staff can help themselves but there must be safeguards against abuse by any users and to prevent residents obtaining access to the machines.

If first aid boxes are not appropriate because of the nature of the work or the layout of the workplace (eg where lone work is carried out) or the work involves a lot of travelling, first aid kits may be a better option. These are designed to be readily portable and will contain basically the same essential items as a first aid box but in smaller quantities because they are designed for personal use.

First aid rooms

These are usually provided where there are more than 400 members of staff, or when there are specific hazards that make a first aid room necessary, or when no accident and emergency facilities are readily available locally.

In care homes there is possibly more of an argument for providing a first aid room for the residents than for the staff, but there is no reason why it should not be used for both.

If a first aid room is provided, it should be readily accessible to ambulance services and be close to toilet facilities. There should be enough space for access by wheelchairs and stretchers. The room should be under the specific charge of a designated person (eg the first aider or 'appointed person': see below) who must ensure that it is kept clean and fully stocked. Ventilation, heating and lighting must also be adequate.

The recommended items for a first aid room include:

- sink with hot and cold running water
- suitable supply of drinking water
- couch and pillow
- soap and paper towels
- smooth work surfaces
- first aid items as in a standard first aid box
- chair
- suitable and sufficient storage facilities for all the equipment
- personal protective clothing (eg waterproof aprons, disposable gloves for the first aiders)
- lidded refuse receptacles – with appropriate refuse sacks
- bowl
- names of all the first aiders and the appropriate contact details
- record book

All structures, furnishings and fittings in first aid rooms must be easy to clean, and the room itself must be readily identifiable.

Keeping a first aid record book is not a legal requirement, although it is good practice. The record of first aid given should include details of the injured person – name and address etc; their occupation; date and time of the incident/injury; details of the accident, any injuries and treatment provided; date of the record and the signature of the person making the entry.

FIRST AIDERS

As well as first aid equipment and facilities, employers must also provide properly trained first aiders to administer first aid treatments.

First aiders must attend and pass a four-day HSE-approved training course. They must also attend and pass a refresher course every three years in order to retain their first aid certificate. There are exceptions to this where there are medically qualified people available who hold qualifications acceptable to the HSE. Confirmation must be obtained from HSE that alternative arrangements are acceptable.

If the work involves particular risks, additional, specialised training may also be required.

There is no set ratio for the number of first aiders to the number of staff, but the ACOP issued with the 1981 Regulations suggests that there should be a minimum of one first aider per 50 members of staff in low-risk businesses, and that this ratio increases as the number of staff and/or the risks increase. A risk assessment should be carried out to determine whether you need to provide a fully trained first aider or if an 'appointed person' is sufficient compliance. The general opinion is that a trained first aider should be provided, and this may be particularly so if first aid treatment is extended to the residents.

First aiders must be around at all times when there are staff at work, so, if you operate 24 hours a day, as most care homes will, there has to be a first aider available 24 hours a day too.

'Appointed persons' support first aiders and may be responsible for 'topping up' first aid boxes. They must also call for medical assistance and take charge of a situation in the temporary absence of a first aider. This does not include times when the first aider is on leave: another first aider must be made available for such times. If an 'appointed person' has been trained in emergency first aid procedures, they may administer them if necessary.

People who are selected to become first aiders must be calm and able to cope authoritatively in stressful situations; they must also be able to leave their jobs quickly and safely in order to attend any incident.

KEY POINTS

- Employers are obliged to provide adequate and appropriate first aid resources for staff at work. In care homes the management should also think about providing first aid treatment to the residents.

- 'Adequate' and 'appropriate' include taking account of the number of employees, the nature and associated risks of the business, the size and distribution of the business and the accessibility of external accident and emergency services.

- 'First aid resources' include first aid boxes, and if necessary first aid kits and first aid rooms, and trained first aiders and appointed persons.

- All first aid arrangements, including any subsequent changes, should be known by staff.

Relevant guidance

COP42 *First aid at work – ACOP*. Available from HSE Books (see p 176).

9 Personal protective equipment

The provision of personal protective equipment (PPE) is an acceptable control measure if the risks cannot be controlled by any other means – PPE is the last resort. PPE is mentioned in specific Regulations (such as COSHH) but it is also covered by the Personal Protective Equipment at Work Regulations 1992. These apply to all work activities, regardless of the type of hazard, and they apply to safety risks as well as health risks.

In care homes, PPE will be significant in connection with the control measures needed after you have made the risk assessment required by the Management of Health and Safety at Work Regulations 1992 (see Chapter 2).

This chapter discusses the requirements of the Personal Protective Equipment at Work Regulations 1992, and some other issues such as the employer not charging for any special protective equipment provided.

Personal Protective Equipment at Work Regulations 1992

These Regulations define PPE as anything designed to be held or worn in order to protect against one or more risks. However, uniforms (as required under food safety laws), work clothing not worn to offer protection against risks, crash helmets required by road traffic law and sports equipment are all excluded.

Suitability

When risks cannot be controlled by other means, employers must provide suitable PPE; self-employed people have to provide their own. PPE will be considered suitable if:

- it is appropriate and effective for the risks it is intended to control;
- it is suitable for the environment where it is intended to be used, taking into account the work environment, the need for communication and any relevant ergonomic factors such as strenuous physical activity, restricted space etc;
- it is adjustable so that it fits the user properly and comfortably.

It should also comply with any relevant EC 'product' Directives (the supplier or manufacturer will be able to confirm this).

In ensuring the suitability of PPE, employers must also assess all the health and safety risks that cannot be controlled by other means, define the characteristics required for the PPE to be effective against those risks and compare those characteristics with actual PPE. It is also important to assess any risks created by the PPE; for example, protective gloves may affect the wearer's ability to grip a load securely. This will also be important if more than one type of PPE has to be worn at once (eg protective goggles and ear protectors may be necessary for some gardening activities, such as 'strimming'); in such a case both have to be compatible and achieve their required levels of protection. As with all assessments, the use of PPE should be reviewed regularly and revised if necessary.

Maintenance and storage accommodation

PPE should be maintained in good working order and in good repair to ensure it remains efficient. Maintenance under the 1992 Regulations includes cleaning. There must also be enough storage space for the PPE when it is not in use.

Information, instruction and training

Employees should understand the risks that the PPE is designed to protect against and appreciate any limits to its effectiveness. They must also know how to use the PPE correctly, including any adjustments necessary to ensure a proper fit. The information, instruction and training provided must be understandable to all the staff, so in some cases foreign language translations and/or pictograms may be necessary if English is not their first language.

Use, loss and faults

When PPE is provided, employers must ensure that it is worn properly and returned to the designated storage place after use.

Employees must use any PPE provided in accordance with the information, instructions and training provided and return it to the designated storage accommodation after use.

Losses or defects/faults must be reported immediately so that replacement PPE can be issued if necessary.

Charges

Section 9 of HASAWA prohibits employers charging for any PPE when it is specifically required under any health and safety laws. This includes items supplied under the Personal Protective Equipment at Work Regulations 1992 if the risk assessment required under the 1992 'Management' Regulations identifies PPE as a necessary control measure because the risks cannot be adequately controlled by other means.

PPE in care homes

It is unlikely that PPE will be a significant issue in most of the work associated with care homes. Examples of when it may be necessary include:

- gloves to protect against contact with chemicals or blood and other body fluids;
- gloves and waterproof aprons for the carers and laundry workers to protect against direct contact with soiled clothing etc;
- eye and/or ear protection when some gardening or maintenance equipment is used (eg strimmers or lathes);
- thermal/waterproof clothing for work done outside;
- oven gloves in the kitchen to protect against burns;
- goggles may be necessary when using or handling some chemicals.

In many cases the PPE will probably be disposable, so the requirement to keep it clean will not apply. When PPE is re-usable it should be regularly maintained and cleaned, to ensure that it remains efficient. It should not be used after its recommended safe life (as defined by the manufacturer). Where possible, PPE should be issued to each individual and should not be shared unless strict cleaning procedures are followed.

If there are any signs of weakness or if maintenance checks detect a fault, the PPE should be replaced, the faulty item being removed from use and disposed of.

KEY POINTS

- PPE should be provided only as a last resort if the risks identified in the risk assessment cannot be adequately controlled by other means.
- PPE provided must be suitable for the risk(s) it is intended to control, taking into account the risk, the working environment, the work itself, the wearer and any ergonomic (working) restrictions.
- Storage space must be provided for PPE not in use; staff must return PPE to this storage after use.
- Employees must be provided with information, instructions and training in how to use the PPE, what risks it is intended to control and any limitations or restrictions on its use. PPE must be used in accordance with this training.
- Employers may not charge for any PPE required under any health and safety legislation.

Relevant guidance

L25 *Personal protective equipment at work – guidance on Regulations*

IND(G)174L *Personal protective equipment at work* (single copies free)

Both the above are available from HSE Books (see p 176).

10 Electricity, gas and water

Although the supply and general safety of electricity, gas and water are well established and very much taken for granted, there are inherent dangers associated with each that require careful control in the workplace.

The dangers associated with electricity, such as electrocution, electric shocks and fire, are well recognised but still account for many work-related accidents each year. It is perhaps a problem of over-familiarity and over-confidence, and is made even more difficult to control where unsafe practices are regularly carried on away from work and then have to be corrected during work time.

The dangers associated with gas and water are perhaps less obvious. Everyone is aware that the misuse of gas may lead to explosion and fire but fortunately these are very rare events. However, there is an even greater danger which is only now being recognised as a serious problem, and that is the release of carbon monoxide gas from the poor combustion of gas in badly maintained gas appliances and/or badly ventilated rooms.

With water there is a serious risk of colonisation with *Legionella* bacteria in poorly maintained water systems. Early associations tended to link Legionnaires' disease with air conditioning plant, although in reality there are several other outlets such as spa baths, whirlpool baths and shower heads – basically any situation where warm water can be present as an aerosol spray.

This chapter looks at the dangers associated with these three services in the context of care homes, and considers the relevant legal rules. (The supply of these services to care homes is outside the scope of this publication and is not discussed.)

ELECTRICITY

The dangers of electricity are well known, yet it is still abused to a considerable extent, resulting in many unnecessary accidents.

The use of electricity at work is covered by the Electricity at Work Regulations 1989. These are designed to prevent danger arising from work on or near electricity. This covers integral building wiring systems as well as portable and fixed electrical appliances.

Standards and recommendations for building wiring systems are governed by the Institution of Electrical Engineers (IEE) 'Regulations for electrical installations' (Wiring Regulations), 16th edition. These are not statutory Regulations (ie law) but are a recognised British Standard (BS 7671:1992) and represent current good practice. Following these recommendations will show that the user is also following the 1989 'Electricity' Regulations.

Portable equipment (eg washing machines, irons, vacuum cleaners, electric lawn mowers, food preparation equipment) generally includes anything that can be plugged in, whether or not it can be physically carried (eg washing machines). Electrical system components such as plugs and sockets are also included in the 1989 Regulations.

Under these Regulations you must define all foreseeable risks associated with any electrical work. This means you will have to consider the suitability of the electrical systems and equipment and decide what preventive or protective measures are needed. You must also consider whether the work with electricity gives rise to danger to other people nearby.

Suitability

In considering the suitability of electrical systems and equipment you need to bear in mind the design, construction, siting and installation in relation to the intended use: for example, all power points should be at least 1.25 metres from a water source, to prevent simultaneous contact with electricity *and* water. (Installation should be carried out by a competent person.) The environmental conditions must also be considered; for example, when electrical equipment is used in wet areas or outside, it must be designed and constructed for that type of use. 'Suitability' also means considering the required performance standards; for example, many domestic appliances such as vacuum cleaners and microwave ovens are unsuitable for heavy commercial use and will be uneconomical, unreliable and possibly unsafe (eg by overheating and catching fire or short circuiting).

When considering the suitability of systems and equipment, associated functions, such as maintenance, servicing, testing and repairs, must be taken into account.

Preventive and protective measures

Safe systems of work and competent persons

Defined safe systems of work are very important, so staff should be trained in the correct use of all electrical appliances and be aware of the associated dangers. Equally important, they should understand that repairs – even simple operations such as fitting plugs or changing fuses (even if they carry these out in their own homes) – must be done by the designated competent person (eg a qualified electrician) at work. Residents must not do their own repairs.

Visual checks

Many problems with electrical cables, plugs and sockets can be picked up in the early stages by encouraging staff to carry out quick visual checks on the appliances they intend to use, before they use them. This should detect worn or loose cables, broken plugs or sockets, and signs of scorching from previous use. These can then be repaired before any incident occurs.

Multiple adaptors

These are potentially very dangerous pieces of equipment and their use should be avoided at all times. The main problem with multiple adaptors is that they lead to overloading of the socket – which may short out and become 'live' or may catch fire. As discussed under 'Fuses', below, electrical sockets for plugging in equipment are usually 13 amps – this is the maximum loading that can be used safely in each socket. As soon as this is exceeded, there is a serious risk of fire or other fault.

The use of multiple adaptors encourages the use of additional appliances in one socket. It would be safe to plug in up to four 3 amp appliances (eg TVs, stereos, table lamps) because this would give a total loading of 12 amps, which is below the 13 amp maximum. However, as soon as a TV (3 amp), a table lamp (3 amp) and a kettle (10 amp) are used together, the total loading is 16 amp, which is above the maximum loading. The problem in allowing the use of multiple adaptors lies in controlling what is plugged into them. It is therefore preferable to prohibit their use and follow the 'one socket – one plug' rule.

If additional socket outlets are required, it is possible for extension blocks to be used (they usually contain a block of four extra sockets) which plug into the mains socket. These are especially designed to give 13 amp loading at each additional outlet and may be used safely to extend the number of available sockets, provided that none of the additional sockets exceeds 13 amps loading.

Extension leads

Extension leads are required to allow electrical appliances to be used at a distance from the initial supply socket. For example, many gardening tasks involving electrical equipment will call for an extension lead. Generally there is no problem with these leads provided they are regularly inspected, tested and looked at carefully before use. There is one well recognised hazard, however, which is associated with rewindable leads: they must be unwound to their full extent, even if only some of the cable is required for the work, in order to prevent them overheating and catching fire.

'Live work'

There may be some situations when it will be necessary for work to be carried out on 'live' electrical equipment. Obviously this should be avoided whenever possible but, if it is necessary, safe systems of work will be very important.

Under the 'Electricity' Regulations work may be done on 'live' equipment only if three conditions are met:

- it is unreasonable in all the circumstances for the electricity to be disconnected;

- it is reasonable in all circumstances for the work to be carried out 'live';
- suitable precautions are taken to prevent injury.

When such work is necessary in care homes (which is unlikely), a competent person should be employed to do the work. This person will also probably follow established safe practices and safety requirements, and you should work together to ensure the safety of everyone in the home. The responsibility is on you to determine the competence of any person you appoint or employ: membership of an appropriate professional organisation and professional qualifications are good indicators but you are advised to confirm these with the respective bodies.

Safety devices

Fuses

There are several practical and inexpensive safety devices that give effective control over electrical hazards. The most common is probably the fuse, which is fitted into each electrical plug. Fuses are of different sizes (and are colour coded accordingly) depending on the power rating of the appliance to be protected. The total number of amps for all equipment plugged into a mains socket must not exceed the amp rating for that socket. In most, but not all, cases the rating for mains sockets is 13 amps. The fuse rating for some of the integral building wiring (eg the mains supply for electric ovens) may be up to 60 amps. The following list gives the power rating on common items of electrical equipment and their required fuse ratings:

televisions, stereos, table lamps, videos, drills, hedge trimmers	up to 750 watts	3 amp	red
toasters, vacuum cleaners	up to 1250 watts	5 amp	black
irons	up to 1750 watts	7 amp	black
kettles	up to 2500 watts	10 amp	black
microwave ovens, washing machines, dishwashers	up to 3000 watts	13 amp	brown

These figures are only a general guide and it is important to check the manufacturers' information and instructions to confirm the power rating and associated fuses. For any electrical equipment purchased, always confirm with the manufacturer or competent person that the fuses fitted are correct – do not assume the seller has it right.

NOTE Although electrical fuses are colour coded, the fuses for 5, 7 and 10 amp are all black so you need to confirm the actual size by checking the size marking on the fuse itself.

Other safety devices

In addition to the fuses incorporated into electrical systems and equipment, there are several other safety devices, including residual circuit (or current) breakers (RCBs) which detect minute electrical leakages going to earth and immediately trip the system (ie cut off the power supply to the appliance). The appliance plugs into the RCB which then plugs into the electric socket. RCBs usually have integrated test buttons and it is important that the device is tested before each use, and is in the 'on' position while the equipment is in use. RCBs are often used with outdoor equipment such as electric lawn mowers, strimmers and hedge cutters where there is a risk of cutting the power cable or wet conditions. Current breakers may also be part of the integrated building wiring system, where they will work like the ones used with portable equipment.

Earthing

Earthing is most commonly associated with the integral building electrical systems and basically provides a route for 'stray' electrical current to go safely into the ground as opposed to making any touching or nearby surfaces or equipment 'live'. All plumbing accessories (eg sinks) will be earthed, as will metal work surfaces such as are found in kitchens. Portable equipment is not always earthed.

Insulation

All electric cables are insulated to prevent contact with any of the conducting surfaces. There are also special insulating tools and protective clothing available for work with electricity.

Maintenance, testing, inspection and record keeping

The 'Electricity' Regulations require electrical systems and equipment to be maintained in order to prevent any dangers arising from their use. The maintenance should be of sufficient quality and frequency to prevent these dangers: you need to consider a planned preventive maintenance regimen for your electrical equipment.

For fixed electrical installations and systems, five-yearly inspections are considered appropriate but the age and condition of the premises will affect this. Most portable equipment should be checked and inspected by a competent person at least once a year. In some cases you may decide that equipment particularly at risk, such as gardening appliances and other equipment subjected to heavy duty use, should be checked more often (eg every six months). In some cases, especially for earthed equipment such as kettles, a combined inspection *and* test procedure will be needed to ensure continued safety. Free leaflet IND(G)160L has a table of frequencies for inspections and testing.

You will also need procedures for checking the safety of any portable electrical equipment that is brought in and used by residents; these should all be included in your annual inspections.

Many organisations stick small labels on equipment that has been inspected to show that it was found to be satisfactory: the dates of the last and next inspections are usually given as well.

There is no requirement in the Regulations to keep maintenance or other records, but if you do so you will be better able to show that you are taking proper precautions.

GAS

The dangers of fire and explosion associated with gas are well known and generally there are satisfactory procedures in place to prevent or at least minimise these events. It is only recently that another problem has been equally widely recognised: this is the risk of carbon monoxide poisoning. Compliance with the relevant legal rules together with good work practices should minimise the risks of any of these dangers occurring in your home.

Legislation

There are several Regulations that cover different aspects of gas safety; for example, the supply of gas from British Gas and defining minimum standards and/or criteria for gas fittings and appliances.

The main Regulations of concern in care homes are the Gas Safety (Installation and Use) Regulations 1994, as amended by the Gas Safety (Installation and Use) (Amendment) Regulations 1996: these are aimed at protecting against risks from gas supplied through mains systems and gas storage vessels. Under these Regulations employers may use only 'specified persons' to carry out any gas-related work: in practice, this means someone who has the appropriate HSE approval – they are members of the Council of Registered Gas Installers (CORGI).

Most of these Regulations relate to the safe installation of gas fittings, meters and appliances. Such work should be dealt with by the person or organisation carrying out the installation. It is up to you, however, to ensure that the various requirements are met: you need to be able to prove the competence of the installers.

Some rules are important to care home owners and managers. The 'responsible person' for the premises (usually the occupier or owner or someone acting with appropriate authority) must prohibit the use of any unsafe appliances if they are aware of (or suspect) any of the following unsafe conditions:

- There is insufficient air supply to allow proper combustion of the gas or to provide sufficient oxygen for breathing.
- The products of combustion are not, or cannot, be safely removed.
- There are gas leaks.
- The fitting or appliance is so faulty or defective that it cannot be used safely.

If any of these unsafe conditions is discovered by installers, they are legally required to notify the 'responsible person' in writing: it is a criminal offence for that appliance or system to continue to be used. Despite this, the installer has no power to isolate the appliance without the 'responsible person's' permission. In extreme cases the installer may notify the gas supplier about an unsafe appliance when it has not been possible to obtain the 'responsible person's' authorisation to repair, modify or replace it. When British Gas is the supplier, it has a right of entry under the Gas Safety (Rights of Entry) Regulations 1983 to disconnect the appliance. When the supplier is not British Gas, there may be some contractual right of disconnection but this cannot be assumed to be the case.

Employers and/or owners must also ensure that any gas appliances, pipework or fittings installed in a place of work are properly maintained in a safe condition. This means that the appliance and associated flues must be inspected for safety once a year by a CORGI-approved competent person, and appropriate records must be kept.

If there is a gas leak, the employer must shut off the gas supply and notify the gas supplier immediately, especially if the leak persists after the supply is shut off. The supply should not be re-opened until a 'competent person' has confirmed that it is safe to do so.

Practices

Staff training in the dangers associated with gas is very important, and all staff should be aware of the correct procedures to follow in an emergency. This should include a knowledge of the appropriate 'shut-off' controls and the procedure laid down in the home for obtaining competent assistance.

The actions of the residents must also be considered, so your procedures should include measures to prevent residents from smoking if a gas leak is detected or suspected.

The symptoms of carbon monoxide poisoning should be explained to all staff and the appropriate first aid treatment must be included in your first aider training. Carbon monoxide detectors may be easily purchased at any major DIY retailers and should be fixed close to each gas appliance in the home. Regular (eg daily) monitoring of these detectors is very important.

WATER

Employers must provide a wholesome supply of drinking water for employees at work (see Chapter 4). Generally, the water supply in the UK is of a very high standard and there are relatively few incidents that pose a health risk. Cold water drawn directly from a pressurised main supply should cause no problems. There may be problems, however, if the cold water is drawn from a tanked supply within or local to the building. When cold taps are not used frequently, and water is thus allowed to stand for a time within the pipework, it is advisable to run the water for a few moments to allow the water to clear. Water left standing in pipes will warm up to the ambient temperature which, in care homes, is usually quite warm. Cold water pipes should always run below hot pipes so that there is no heat gain from the hot pipes to the cold.

The main problem is colonisation of the water system by *Legionella* bacteria which cause Legionnaires' disease. This is a type of pneumonia caused by breathing in infected droplets or aerosols of water, although there can also be serious effects on other body organs. Most cases are associated with people between 40 and 70 years of age but there are susceptible groups outside these limits, such as smokers, alcoholics and people with cancer or chronic respiratory or kidney diseases. Men are also more susceptible than women. Care homes are likely to have particularly susceptible residents.

Legionnaires' disease is often associated with air conditioning plant, but in practice there are many potential exposure points. These include any situation where hot/warm water is present in droplet or aerosol form, such as in shower heads, spa baths and whirlpool baths. The risk posed by *Legionella* bacteria in a water system is dealt with by the COSHH Regulations (see Chapter 6).

Legionella bacteria are known to favour temperatures of between 20°C and 45°C for growth, so if you ensure that temperatures are outside these limits you have some means of control. Hot water storage should be maintained at 60°C, while hot water distribution should give a temperature of 50°C at the point of use within one minute of the tap being turned on. However, a water temperature of 50°C at the outlet is liable to cause scalding and must be controlled by hot-water cut-offs or mixer controls so that the water drawn from the system is at a safer 43°C. (See Chapter 12 on the safety of residents in relation to water temperatures.) Cold water storage and distribution should be at 20°C or less.

Apart from using the temperature of the water as a means of control it is also important to undertake regular maintenance of the water system, especially cleaning, flushing out 'dead legs' in the pipework (areas where water may remain for long periods) and ensuring that foreign matter cannot get into any of the tanks or pipes and overflows. Disinfection may also be achieved by thermal heat purging the system or chemical treatment. Relevant advice on maintaining your water system should be readily available from a reputable plumber.

Local authorities must keep a register of all cooling towers in their district, so you must notify your authority if your home has a cooling tower or evaporative condenser installed.

KEY POINTS

- Dangers arising from work with or near electricity must be prevented: 'electricity' includes electrical equipment, appliances and fixed electrical installations, such as building wiring systems.
- The dangers can be prevented by making sure that any equipment is suitable for the intended task and the conditions it is likely to be exposed to, and by providing suitable safety devices.
- Portable electrical appliances should be inspected at least once a year; more frequently if they are used a lot and/or pose a particular risk.
- Fixed installations should be inspected at least every five years.
- Gas work must be undertaken only by CORGI-approved people.
- All gas appliances, fittings etc must be suitable for the intended use, well maintained and used in properly ventilated areas.
- Water systems, especially where there is warm water or where water droplets or aerosols are likely to be produced at the point of use, must be regularly maintained to make sure that the colonisation and growth of *Legionella* bacteria are prevented.
- It is essential to have procedures to assess and control the risks posed by any of these services to the residents, as well as to the staff.

Relevant guidance

HS(R)25 *Memorandum of guidance on the Electricity at Work Regulations 1989*

HS(G)85 *Electricity at work – safe working practices*

HS(G)107 *Maintaining portable and transportable electrical equipment*

IND(G)160L *Maintaining portable electrical equipment in offices* (single copies free)

IND(G)164L *Maintaining portable electrical equipment in hotels* (single copies free)

L56 *Safety in the installation and use of gas systems and appliances: ACOP*

IND(G)79 *Gas appliances – keep them serviced, keep them safe* (single copies free)

L8 *The prevention or control of legionellosis (including Legionnaires' disease): ACOP*

HS(G)70 *The control of legionellosis, including Legionnaires' disease*

All the above are available from HSE Books (see p 176).

Institution of Electrical Engineers – Regulations for electrical installations, 16th edition ('Wiring' Regulations). This is available from IEE, PO Box 26, Hitchin, Herts, SG5 1SA; or from the British Standards Institution (BSI) (address on p 176), which supplies it at half price to BSI members.

11 Occupational health issues

Apart from exposure to hazardous substances, there are several other issues that may lead to work-related health (as opposed to safety) problems, and they need to be considered under the remit of health and safety as a whole and dealt with by your risk assessments.

This chapter discusses the main issues of smoking, stress, shiftwork and hours of work, drug and alcohol abuse, and blood-borne diseases. Occupational health techniques such as health screening and health surveillance are also discussed. Display screen work (VDUs) is dealt with in Chapter 5.

All occupational health issues that relate to identifiable individuals must be treated as highly confidential: this is extremely important in gaining the confidence of staff in implementing your home's policies.

SMOKING

Of all health and safety issues this is probably the most emotive to staff and may be compounded in care homes by the rights of residents to smoke in what is essentially their own home.

When dealing with the problems of smoking there are two matters to be considered: first, fire risks due to careless disposal of cigarette ends and matches (see Chapter 13); secondly, health risks from inhaling tobacco smoke, particularly where this is involuntary (as in 'passive smoking').

Despite increasing evidence that passive smoking damages health, with the exception of the 'Workplace' Regulations (which require non-smokers to be protected from tobacco smoke in rest areas), there is no explicit legal rule that deals with smoking at work from a health point of view.

Some lawyers think that there is a duty to protect non-smokers from the effects of tobacco smoke under section 2 of HASAWA (see Chapter 1). This has not yet been tested in the courts, except in the case of an asthma sufferer who had clearly recognisable and directly linked health problems several times after being exposed to tobacco smoke at work. In general, however, it is very difficult to prove that health problems arise solely because of workplace exposure to smoke (as opposed to exposure during social or other activities).

Even so, it is likely that an employer would have some duty to protect non-smokers at work, if only from a comfort point of view.

Smoking policies

There are obvious occasions when smoking has to be expressly prohibited at work: for example, in food preparation work (under the food safety laws) and where flammable substances are present.

In most other work situations, employers are increasingly implementing 'smoking policies' at work, which usually reflect the views of the majority of the staff. In introducing such a policy it is important for everyone to know what all the choices are in any ballot, what they mean in practice, and how the final decision will be made (eg by simple majority voting). Full consultation at all times is very important if the policy you finally introduce is going to be accepted and followed by your staff. The main choices include:

- a total ban throughout the premises;
- a ban in all workplaces but with designated smoking areas made available;
- an informal agreement among staff in their particular work areas.

The rights and opinions of the residents must also be taken into account, both from the point of view of residents smoking in what will be workplaces for the staff and, conversely, the effects on the residents of staff who smoke. One other factor to be considered is that smokers tend to have a strong smell of tobacco on themselves and on their clothes: this may be unpleasant for residents who require close personal contact for their care.

As with any policy, it is important that staff be fully aware of what they are required, or not required, to do. This should be achieved if there has been full and proper consultation. A disciplinary procedure should be laid down for cases when the policy is not followed by a member of staff.

Some employers ease the introduction of their smoking policies for the staff by providing appropriate support facilities (eg counselling, education) to help staff give up smoking.

HOURS OF WORK AND SHIFTWORK

Care work, by definition and implication, involves members of staff being available around the clock. The nature of the work obviously varies depending on the level and degree of care offered to (or needed by) the residents. This 24-hour presence has two major points of interest in health and safety:

- the number of hours worked by employees;
- the timing and duration of the shift patterns worked in the home.

At present there are no specific legal duties regarding hours of work or shiftwork (except for lorry drivers, pilots, and the like), although excessive hours and/or unsuitable shift patterns that pose a risk to health do come under section 2 of HASAWA – the general duty to ensure the health and safety of staff, so far as is reasonably practicable.

A European Directive that defines minimum periods of rest, night work, annual leave and maximum weekly hours, and addresses the effects of repetitive/monotonous work now looks almost certain to become law, despite the UK's challenge, in the European Court of Justice, to its implementation. The aspects of the Directive relevant to care homes are:

- A rest period of at least 11 consecutive hours in any 24-hour period.
- An uninterrupted rest period of at least 24 hours in each seven-day period. This is in addition to the 11 hours mentioned above and should, in principle, include Sunday, although this last point will be left to each Member State to decide.

- A daily rest break (duration to be decided between employers and staff) if the working day is more than six hours.
- A maximum working week of 48 hours (including overtime) in every seven-day period.
- Four weeks' minimum paid annual leave (money may not be taken in lieu).
- A maximum of eight hours' night work in a 24-hour period.
- A maximum of eight hours' combined day and night work in a 24-hour period in which the work involves special hazards or significant physical or mental strain.
- Free health assessments for night workers before starting work and at regular intervals thereafter.
- Transfer to suitable day work if health problems arise from night work.
- Notification of regular night work to the competent authority.
- Some night work may be subject to certain conditions.
- Applying the principle of 'fitting the work to the worker' (*not* the worker to the work) in which repetitive/monotonous work is carried out, health and safety issues (such as work breaks) must also be dealt with.

The date specified for implementation is 23 November 1996. Information on further developments relating to the implementation of this Directive should be available from the Department of Trade and Industry (DTI) (Tel: 0171-215 5000).

Hours of work

The length of the shifts that members of staff work is an important health and safety consideration: long hours lead to physical and mental fatigue, making it more difficult for strenuous work to be carried out efficiently and safely, as well as reducing the ability to concentrate.

These effects will be improved or worsened by the number and frequency of breaks permitted and the conditions in the workplace. For example, a humid atmosphere will cause physical fatigue quicker than the same work in a cool, well-ventilated area.

If 'on call' systems are operated in the home, the effects of the extra hours worked by the person 'on call' must be taken into account. Suitable compensation in time off is essential, and should be taken as close as possible to the time the extra hours were worked.

In the current climate of streamlining staffing levels, many employees are increasingly faced with having to cope with the same workload as used to be carried out by a greater number of staff. Stress and depression are increasingly recognised work-related illnesses, and in many cases the cause or aggravating factor is over-work and anxiety about job security (stress is discussed in more detail on p 108). Despite some current perceptions, staff are not (and should not be) an expendable commodity.

If staff have to work long hours, they must have adequate breaks away from the work and adequate rest periods between shifts. The effects on social life, although not a health and safety problem as such, may have an impact on their standard of work.

Frequent or continuous overtime being needed to meet the required standards of care is a serious indicator that staffing levels are insufficient for the volume of work that has to be done, and that staffing levels should be reviewed.

Shiftwork

The human body generally works to a set pattern of activity and rest (eg activity during the day and rest at night). Most work situations follow this pattern by operating 9.00am to 5.00pm (or similar) shifts. If 24-hour cover is required, as in care services, some form of shift system has to be operated. There are basically five shift patterns:

- night shifts;
- morning shifts – from early morning to early afternoon;
- afternoon shifts – from early afternoon to late evening;
- rotating shifts – different shifts are worked on a rota;
- split shifts – an early and a late shift with a free period between.

Of these, the most significant (in health and safety terms) are the night and rotating shifts because they cause most disruption to the natural body cycles. Staff who always work night shifts will usually adjust to this pattern and will be able to work normally. The situation is more complicated with regard to rotating shifts because the body is continually having to re-adjust to active and rest periods at different times. To a certain extent the effects may be reduced by operating extra-long shifts (eg 12 hours over three consecutive periods, followed by four days off). From a health and safety point of view, it is better to keep the shifts constant wherever possible.

The effects of shift work are often associated with reduced and disturbed sleep periods and unusual eating patterns which may lead to a reduction in the actual amount of food consumed. There is also evidence that the intake of caffeine, drugs (sleeping pills) and cigarettes increases during shiftwork as people try to stay awake or induce sleep as appropriate.

It is very important that managers and supervisors recognise and deal with any health problems caused by hours of work or shift patterns. Full consultation with the staff when new shift patterns or work conditions are being considered is very important.

STRESS

Over all industries, stress and depression now comprise one of the most common occupational illnesses, and are clearly covered by section 2 of HASAWA, which requires employers to ensure the health and safety of employees at work, so far as is reasonably practicable (see Chapter 1). 'Health' includes mental as well as physical health, but in some cases the two are very closely connected.

There are two health and safety problems to be dealt with: first, the ill health of staff who suffer from stress owing to pressures of work; and, secondly, the reduced ability of these people to work safely and reliably because of that stress.

Causes

Isolating the precise cause of stress may be very difficult because stress is often affected by many factors, not all of which are work related, even if the stress itself may have work implications. Common causes from private life include bereavement, divorce and moving house; causes of stress at work include too much work, too little work, insufficient control over the work, boring repetitive work, uncertainty of job security and poorly designed workplaces. The threat or actual occurrence of abuse (whether verbal or physical) is another common cause of stress and one that may be relevant in care homes.

Symptoms

Stress is a very individual matter, as some people respond positively to pressure of work whereas others cannot cope and start to become stressed in the same situation. Not only is it the degree of subjection that is variable, but also the precise causative factor. Something that is extremely stressful to one person may be very stimulating to someone else. However, no matter what the trigger is, there are recognisable symptoms associated with stress. It is important for these to be detected by managers and supervisors. The symptoms include:

- poor time keeping;
- frequent sickness absence;
- behavioural changes, including tendencies towards aggression, irritability and eventual withdrawal;
- reduction in concentration and ability to make decisions;
- increased lethargy;
- changes in appearance and habits;
- increased dependency on caffeine, cigarettes, drugs etc;
- spontaneous crying;
- disturbed sleep.

Generally, these will develop over a period of time so it is important for them to be recognised and dealt with quickly.

It is also possible for groups of employees to develop symptoms of stress; these are usually associated with particular problems in their workplace or with work practices. Increased sickness absence can be an indicator of this, as well as a reduction in the standard and/or volume of work done.

Effects of stress

Apart from the health effects of stress there are some other important health and safety issues to be dealt with. Some of the best-recognised symptoms of stress are a reduction in people's ability concentrate, a reduction in memory capacity and increased aggressiveness. These increase the risk of harm not only to the sufferers but also to their colleagues and possibly the residents as well. When dangerous machinery is operated or medicines are administered to residents, the potential for error is increased significantly.

As with smoking, employers may wish to offer support in these cases; this can include counselling as well as training for staff to recognise and control stress within their own limits. Equally important is training for employers so that they can identify and remedy causes of stress in their workplace; this should include encouraging staff to admit that they may be suffering from stress in the first place. Stress is still a condition that people are reluctant to admit to, so the job of identifying and controlling it must be done by the employer.

Do not be fooled into thinking that, just because you are not aware of any stress-related problems in your home, they do not exist.

SUBSTANCE ABUSE

In this book 'substance abuse' means taking intentionally any substance such as alcohol, the vapours from solvents or glue, tranquillisers, as well as the common 'hard' drugs such as heroin and cocaine.

Although substance abuse may not seem directly relevant to health and safety, many employers are drawing up and implementing policies regarding substance abuse for their workplaces. As with all other policies, there should also be a clearly laid down disciplinary procedure for non-compliance.

Given the presence and attractiveness of prescription-only medicines in many care homes, managers should seriously consider introducing such a policy.

Types of substances

The substances most commonly abused may be grouped according to their effect on the body, as follows:

■ Stimulants – which stimulate the body to become more active (eg amphetamines, cocaine, nicotine, caffeine).

■ Depressants – which de-stimulate the body, ie slow the body down; they also reduce the perception of pain (eg heroin, morphine, barbiturates, tranquillisers, alcohol).

■ Deliriants – which cause the brain to become confused (eg glues, solvents, lighter fuels).

■ Hallucinogens – which affect the perception of reality and alter moods (cannabis, LSD).

Other commonly encountered substances include non-prescription pain killers and cough mixtures.

As with stress, external factors may be involved in substance abuse, which employers will have no control over. Because of the serious physical and mental effects caused by deliberate exposure to these substances, the employer can and should lay down acceptable standards of behaviour in the workplace. This is justified because of the health and safety risks, not only to the abuser but also to their colleagues and the residents.

Symptoms and controls

The symptoms of substance abuse are very similar to stress and include:

■ deterioration in time-keeping;

■ sickness absence;

■ changes in behaviour and appearance;

■ irrationality;

■ inability to concentrate;

■ reduction in body co-ordination;

■ constant talking.

It is possible that there will be accompanying physical signs such as needle marks, sore or dilated eyes, smelly breath, sore areas of skin (eg around the mouth and nose). There may also be an increase in crime or theft if money is needed to support the habit.

As the symptoms are so similar to other occupational illnesses, it is important that the cause of the problem is identified so the appropriate action can be taken.

Full consultation with the staff should be undertaken at all stages of setting up such a policy. Any policy statement must state clearly what is expected from the staff and what the consequences of non-compliance will be. The policy should encourage staff taking drugs prescribed by their GPs to report that fact to their manager or supervisor so that they are not inadvertently disciplined for taking proper medication.

Employers are increasingly offering counselling, education and rehabilitation to staff to help them 'kick' the habit.

BLOOD-BORNE DISEASES

Mistakenly, many people consider HIV (Human Immunodeficiency Virus) and AIDS (Acquired ImmunoDeficiency Syndrome) to be the most significant health and safety issue in relation to contact with blood and other body fluids (eg urine, saliva, faeces, semen). In fact, the work-related risk associated with HIV infection is generally very low, although it is slightly higher in the care services.

Hepatitis B (hep B) is a more common condition, especially in homes for people with learning difficulties because the standards of personal hygiene of the residents there are usually lower than in other homes. Increased salivation in some mentally handicapped people, close proximity of staff and other residents may result in an increased susceptibility to this infection.

Although infections with HIV and hepatitis B are totally different, at work they are both associated with direct contact with infected blood or other body fluids via open wounds. Similar control measures therefore apply to both.

Infections arising from contact with infected blood or other body fluids are covered by the COSHH Regulations (see Chapter 6).

HIV and AIDS

AIDS occurs as a result of becoming infected with the HIV virus, but infection with HIV does not automatically lead to full-blown AIDS. The most usual sources of infection are unprotected sex with an infected partner and the use of infected hypodermic needles. The risks of contracting HIV or AIDS at work is really very small, and the main route of infection will be direct contact with infected blood or body fluids.

The virus can be transmitted to an unborn child from an infected mother, and this particular risk must be assessed under the Management of Health and Safety at Work (Amendment) Regulations 1994 (see p 115).

AIDS is usually a slow-developing condition which breaks down the body's defence systems, thus allowing other conditions (such as pneumonia) to develop. AIDS may take years to show itself, and there is no cure at the present time, although some drugs appear to delay its onset.

Hepatitis B

Like HIV, the hepatitis B virus is transmitted by contact with infected blood, nowadays most commonly through unprotected sex or the use of infected hypodermic needles, or by contact with waste body fluids. The virus attacks the liver cells and may lead to cirrhosis or cancer of the liver. One of the problems with this virus is that infected carriers may be asymptomatic (ie not have any symptoms of the disease themselves) but can infect other people. Men tend to be more susceptible than women.

There is an effective vaccine against hepatitis B, so an inoculation programme for staff who are at risk should form part of your control measures to protect against infection. Staff cannot be forced to have the vaccine, so explaining the risks, the effects of the disease and necessary precautions is very important.

Controls

When assessing who is at risk of infection from blood-borne diseases, it is important to consider everyone who may come into contact with infected blood or body fluids. Care staff who are in intimate contact with residents are subjected to some degree of risk but so are laundry workers who handle soiled linen, and domestic staff and refuse collectors may be put at risk if proper disposal procedures are not followed. First aiders may also be at risk if they have to provide first aid treatment to an infected person.

Proper equipment and training must be provided to reduce these risks.

Your health and safety policy should set out the correct procedures to use when there is a possibility of contact with infected blood or other body fluids.

Good standards of personal hygiene are very important in reducing the risk of infection not only to staff but also between residents where more than one resident is cared for by any one member of staff. All open cuts should be cleaned and covered with a suitable waterproof dressing. A procedure should be laid down to ensure that all spillages are cleaned up immediately. The general and COSHH risk assessments (see Chapter 6) should indicate the areas of risk in relation to puncture wounds so that steps can be taken to eliminate them. For example, you may insist on used hypodermic needles being disposed of into the sharps container immediately after use, so that they are not re-sheathed: this reduces the risk of receiving accidental puncture wounds by trying to re-sheath the needles.

Ethics

You cannot insist on your staff undergoing a blood test to check whether they have a blood-borne disease, unless this is clearly included in the terms and conditions of their employment. Your staff also have a right of confidentiality and are under no obligation to inform you if they have such a condition. If they do inform you, you too are bound by the rules of confidentiality.

This whole area is very difficult to manage because employers must protect staff and residents from infection from blood-borne and other diseases but are also tied down by the rules of ethics and confidentiality. In these cases all the employer can do is to take every reasonable measure possible to prevent or at least reduce the risk of infection in all cases.

As far as fitness to work is concerned, the ability of any sufferer to work normally must be kept under regular review. If necessary, a member of staff may have to be moved to other more suitable work. In extreme cases, if no other suitable work is available, the member of staff must be dismissed: this is the last resort and there is no guarantee that the dismissal will be held to be fair in any legal proceedings.

PREGNANT WORKERS AND NURSING MOTHERS

Unlike most other areas of occupational health, the welfare of new and expectant mothers are covered by special rules: they are the Management of Health and Safety at Work (Amendment) Regulations 1994. The 'Workplace' Regulations also require rest facilities to be provided for pregnant women and nursing mothers (see Chapter 4).

The risk assessment carried out under the 1992 'Management' Regulations must include any specific risks to women who are pregnant, or who have given birth within the last six months or who are breast feeding. If any of the risks identified cannot be controlled by altering working practices or working hours, then, where possible, suitable alternative work should be found. If no suitable alternative work is available, it may be necessary to suspend the woman from work (with pay) until she may work safely and without risk to her, or her baby's, health. If the new or expectant mother is employed on night work, she may be suspended from duty if there is a risk to her health and safety, if the employer is given a certificate to that effect, signed by a registered medical practitioner or midwife.

The employer is not obliged to fulfil any of the duties mentioned above unless the new or expectant mother has informed the employer that she is pregnant or nursing a baby, or when the employer has grounds for believing that the woman is no longer pregnant.

The Maternity (Compulsory Leave) Regulations 1994 prohibit employers knowingly employing a woman within two weeks of her having given birth.

Fitness to work

A new or expectant mother is not automatically unfit to work, although special consideration should be given to protecting the health and safety of the woman and/or her baby where they may be at risk from the work.

Pregnancy especially is a changing condition that may alter a woman's ability to perform certain tasks as it progresses. It is therefore important that assessments on pregnant women are reviewed regularly during the term of the pregnancy and the necessary actions taken.

The HSE guidance defines three areas of risk:

- Physical agents such as manual handling, vibration, ionising radiation, poor or prolonged posture.

- Chemical agents, especially those that are known to have harmful genetic or other hereditary effects or which can be passed on to the unborn child (eg lead).

- Biological agents, especially those that cause abortion or miscarriage, infection and/or physical or neurological damage.

The chemical and biological agents have been discussed in general terms in Chapter 6, under the COSHH Regulations.

It is also important to understand and take into account the physiological changes that occur during pregnancy because these will affect a pregnant woman's ability to work. Morning sickness may affect early morning shift work as well as instances where the woman might be exposed to nauseating smells. There may be increasing tiredness as the pregnancy progresses: this will be important where work must be done standing or where particular concentration is needed. Poor or prolonged posture, especially in hot environments, may cause or aggravate varicose veins. There will be an increasing need for the woman to visit the toilet, particularly in the later stages of pregnancy. At that stage the sheer increase in size may hinder safe manual handling techniques.

By being aware of, and dealing with, these changes you can maintain a safe and healthy work environment for new or expectant mothers.

VIOLENCE

Violence should be taken to mean threats, abuse and assault, both physical and verbal. Although physical assault is relatively rare, managers of care homes will almost certainly have to deal with some aspects of violence: verbal abuse and threats are the most likely. The problem is twofold:

■ violence towards staff on the part of residents;

■ violence towards residents on the part of staff (see Chapter 12).

Both must be controlled and dealt with appropriately.

The first stage is to get agreement about what 'violence' means in your home: what are and are not the acceptable standards of behaviour. It is also very important to be able to predict when violence might occur. Situations where cash is handled is an obvious example, as are care work with mentally confused people and work with drug addicts or alcoholics. Work that involves dealing with the public may well expose staff to verbal abuse and threats, especially if the abusers are particularly emotional or agitated.

Staff are commonly reluctant to report incidents of violence, often in the misbelief that they were inadequate in some way. For violence to be treated properly, it is important that all incidents be reported so that an accurate picture of the problem can be established. For example, it may be that apparently unconnected incidents all relate back to one resident – who may be better off in a different kind of environment where the appropriate care and supervision can be provided. Control measures will include trying to prevent hazardous situations arising by ensuring that two members of staff care for residents who are known to have violent tendencies, by avoiding the use of cash, and so on.

It is also important to identify and deal with any potential problem areas within the premises. For example, fitting alarm buttons in order to call for help and installing security lighting to eliminate dark or blind spots. Remote camera surveillance might be considered in extreme cases.

When a member of staff is required to leave the home for work-related appointments there should be a fully logged contact procedure so that the precise movements of that person are known as far as possible. After each meeting there should be confirmation that everything is in order. Other matters to think about include:

- providing mobile phones (and perhaps also vehicle rescue services such as the AA or RAC) for staff who have to work off-site;
- ensuring that staff who work shifts can get to and from work safely (eg by public transport – consider the distance from the transport service to the home);
- parking places being available near to the home;
- the safety of any staff who live on the premises.

Training staff to cope with potentially violent situations is also very important. They will then be confident in dealing with any situation that arises. More importantly, they will know how to defuse dangerous situations.

HEALTH SCREENING AND HEALTH SURVEILLANCE

Health screening

Employers must take account of an individual's capability to perform a job; it therefore follows that some sort of health screening forms part of an employer's responsibilities. Under the Disability Discrimination Act 1995, employers will be expected to take appropriate and reasonable measures *not* to discriminate against disabled people in any employment policies such as recruitment, training, promotion and dismissal. They will also be expected to make necessary and reasonable changes to their workplace in order to accommodate any disabled employees. Although these provisions will apply only to workplaces where there are 20 or more employees, they form the basis of current good practices expected to be followed by all other employers.

The requirement to assess an individual's ability to undertake a certain job will not be affected by the Act when it comes into force (probably from the end of 1996). There are recognised exceptions to some provisions in the Act in relation to health and safety, although these cannot be used as a convenient excuse for not employing a disabled person. Any apparent discriminatory action by an employer may be taken to an Industrial Tribunal.

It is possible to conduct pre-employment health interviews, which should be based on a pre-employment questionnaire in which the candidate is asked specific questions relative to the health requirement of the job. The design and interpretation of these pre-employment (and other) health questionnaires are very important in obtaining relevant information: you may wish to use an occupational health service or consultant to help you in this. First impressions may also be relevant: for example, a candidate with long and dirty fingernails is not an immediate choice for employment as a food handler, and an excessively overweight person may be unable to perform manual handling tasks safely. The process is obviously a lot more complicated and other employment law issues may also be involved (eg various forms of discrimination). It is also worth remembering that the pre-employment health check is only as accurate as the answers provided, and confidentiality on medical issues means that potential employees are not obliged to own up to health problems – with certain exceptions; for example, when being hired for a catering position, they must disclose relevant health information, ideally when applying for the job. If these problems come to light later and pose a significant risk, the employer may be able to take action against the candidate for intentionally providing false information.

There may be benefits for providing a regular health screening service for staff so that problems can be identified and dealt with.

Health surveillance

Very generally, this is the process of watching staff health, either by proper medical supervision or through self-examination by the staff themselves. In many ways it overlaps health screening (discussed above).

The aim of health surveillance is to detect health problems at the earliest stages so that appropriate steps can be taken before the problems become serious.

Advice on all aspects of staff health may be obtained from the Employment Medical Advisers of the HSE, who are located in the HSE area offices (see HSE in your local telephone directory).

- There are well known health risks associated with smoking/passive smoking, hours of work/shiftwork, stress, substance abuse, blood-borne diseases, pregnancy and violence.

- Clearly explained policies for all of these topics should be adopted. Special staff support services (such as counselling) may be necessary in some cases.

- Staff should be fully consulted at all stages if these policies are to be accepted and workable in practice.

- Health screening and health surveillance may be useful in establishing the suitability of a candidate for a job, and in the early detection of any work-related health problems, respectively.

Relevant guidance

HS(G)116 *Stress at work – a guide for employers*

HS(G)122 *New and expectant mothers at work – a guide for employers*

HS(G)137 *Health risk management – a practical guide for managers in small and medium sized enterprises*

Management of occupational health in the health services

Management of occupational health services for healthcare staff

Violence to staff in the health services

IND(G)62L *Protecting your health at work* (single copies free)

IND(G)63L *Passive smoking at work* (single copies free)

IND(G)69L *Violence to staff* (single copies free)

IND(G)129L *Mental distress at work* (single copies free)

All the above are available from HSE Books (see p 176).

12 Residents, contractors and other people

HASAWA places duties on employers to ensure the health and safety of staff at work and of non-employees who may be harmed in some way by the work. Most of this book has concentrated on the risks to staff that may arise during their work, but it is equally important to deal with the risks to your residents and other non-employees that may arise from your work or from situations that you control (eg the condition of the premises).

This chapter discusses the main risks to your residents and how other groups of people may affect the health and safety standards in your home, or for whom you are specially responsible, such as contractors, young people and trainees.

RESIDENTS

In most cases the steps you take to protect your staff will also protect your residents. A most important step in safeguarding the health and safety of your residents comes when you assess their physical and mental abilities and/or disabilities, and are able to gauge their level of understanding of dangers in and around the home.

Physically and mentally fit residents will probably pose fewer problems than residents who are physically disabled, mentally ill or with a learning disability. They will be able to understand and react to dangerous situations even though they may show a stronger sense of independence – which itself will need to be taken into account.

Residents who are especially at risk should be known as such to all staff: they, in turn, should know the correct procedures for dealing with any problems that may arise.

There are basic and general rules that can be applied to protect residents; examples are:

- keeping all work equipment and substances in secure stores when they are not in use;
- planning work so that it is done when residents are in other parts of the home;
- preventing access to dangerous areas (such as kitchens);
- ensuring that all spillages are cleaned up immediately;
- ensuring that corridors, stairs etc are always kept clear of obstructions;
- ensuring that there are good levels of lighting, especially where there is a change in floor level;
- ensuring that window restrictors are placed on openable windows where there is a risk of residents falling out.

Particular disabilities will have to be taken into account, especially in emergencies. For example, it may be necessary to provide braille signs on escape routes so that residents with poor eyesight can escape from the home independently if necessary. Residents with poor hearing may need visual or vibrating emergency signals to tell them that there is an emergency. Residents with impaired mobility may require handrails and ramps, and may need help if there is an evacuation. The normal effects of old age must also be thought about.

In addition to these general points, there are several other factors which, although not directly related to work activities, can seriously affect the health and safety of residents.

Water temperatures and hot surfaces
Water temperature

There have been well publicised cases in which residents have been severely scalded, and even killed, by getting into baths containing very hot water. In most of these cases inadequate supervision of the bath being filled and inadequate checking of the water before the residents got into the bath were contributory factors: both types of problem resulted from poor health and safety management and control in the home. Some of these cases have led to criminal charges followed by claims of negligence and awards of compensation being made against the home.

When residents cannot determine the danger from hot water, there is a greater responsibility on the home to ensure that they do not come to any harm. This means that staff must ensure that the residents in question are properly supervised at all bath times, and that there must be controls on the taps so that hot water cannot be drawn off on its own. Controlling the temperature at the outlet point is also possible: a maximum of 43°C is considered acceptable, but this should not be allowed to interfere with temperature controls used to prevent the growth of *Legionella* bacteria. Water temperatures over 50°C are accepted as creating a risk of scalding, the risk increasing as the temperature increases. Regular maintenance is needed to make sure that the controls remain effective.

When a 'near as possible normal domestic environment' is required (eg in rehabilitation units), supervision will be an essential control measure but it can be supplemented with the use of 'VERY HOT WATER' warning labels on all hot water outlets.

In deciding appropriate control measures, the residents' frailties and their ability to protect themselves from scalding must be weighed against their right to have hot baths. In general the greater the risk, the more you will be expected to do to control it.

Surface temperatures

Residents may also suffer severe burns from hot surfaces such as radiators, certain panel type fires and exposed hot pipework. The highest accepted surface temperature is 43°C when the system is operating on maximum output. Discussions with the manufacturer of any such products may lead to more appropriate appliances.

Other ways of controlling the surface temperature include:

- guarding the hot surface to prevent contact;
- using special low surface temperature heat emitters;
- reducing the flow temperature.

Again, the frailties and abilities of residents must be assessed.

Drugs administration and security

It is quite likely that some residents will be taking prescribed medicines or drugs, and the correct administration and ultimate security of these substances are significant health and safety factors (see also Chapter 11).

Administration

It is essential that residents receive the drugs or medicines that they have been prescribed and at the correct times; for example, a resident with diabetes requires regular insulin injections. Failure to achieve these requirements may have dire consequences.

The Misuse of Drugs Act 1971 requires 'controlled substances' (listed in the Schedule to that Act) to be kept in a secure cabinet or cupboard and a drugs register must be kept on the premises. The register should show the date of all drug purchases, the amounts purchased, batch numbers, the supplier's details, and all consequent distribution (eg for residents' use).

Prescribed medicines should be administered only by an appropriately qualified medical person (a nurse or doctor), who will be responsible for calculating and preparing the correct dosage and seeing that it is properly administered. Drugs rounds should always be undertaken by at least two people so that there is confirmation on such matters as the correct dosage. All medicines administered to residents should be recorded, the time, date and dosage given being noted and the record signed by the person responsible.

Residents may be able to administer their own medicine if your assessment indicates that there is no significant risk in their doing so, but all such medicines should still be kept in a central secure unit and not left under the control of the resident. The practical, day-to-day aspects of residents' medicines are discussed in Age Concern's *Health Care in Residential Homes* (see p 180).

If mistakes are made, it is important for proper medical advice to be sought as soon as the mistake is discovered so that remedial or precautionary measures can be taken quickly. It is important to record any such mistakes.

Storage and stock control

All medicines should be kept in secure units and should be handled only by properly authorised people, who will have received training in the home's procedures for handling drugs. There should be a procedure for signing in and out the key to the secure unit and for recording any medicines removed, including their intended purpose.

Weekly checks should be made on all medicine stocks to ensure that the correct storage conditions are in force and that there is no deterioration in the stock held. If there is any doubt about the quality of a product, dispose of it immediately: never use anything that causes you concern. All products will have a data sheet which will provide relevant information on use, storage and disposal.

Arrangements should be made for obtaining emergency supplies (eg when there is an urgent, unpredicted need for a certain drug). This may be done by establishing a relationship with a local pharmacist who is willing to deliver the medicines needed.

Disposal

The best method is to have an arrangement with your pharmacist for unwanted medicines to be returned to them for disposal: get a receipt for all drugs that are returned. If it is not possible to return them to the pharmacist, they may be disposed of by incineration but details of the medicines and quantities involved may be needed for disposal licence purposes. Similarly, the descriptions and quantities of toxic or otherwise dangerous drugs will often have to be provided so that waste disposal contractors can obey the environmental and waste disposal laws. As a last resort, medicines can be disposed of in the drains but there are strict laws and penalties governing this. Before using this method, it is essential to contact your local authority because there are considerable regional variations in the regulations and conditions to be met.

Remember that you are responsible for ensuring the safe and proper disposal of any drugs or medicines, so you are also responsible for making sure of the competence of any contractor you use.

The local waste regulation authority will be able to provide more information on local services.

OUTSIDE ACTIVITIES AND RESIDENTS' RIGHTS

The rights of residents to their freedom is a very important issue that has close links with health and safety. If residents have full physical and mental abilities, there is no reason why they cannot safely enjoy complete freedom. It may be necessary to warn them of any hazards they might encounter and how to deal with them, or even to provide a supervisory escort; but on the whole they will be able to deal with any situation that might arise.

When outside trips, visits and activities (eg barbecues) for the residents are organised by the care home, you must assess the suitability of the residents to attend each particular event so as to ensure their health and safety (and that of others) while they are away. The assessment should include discussion with the resident about the hazards associated with the activity and any difficulty they may experience. In extreme cases, where it is felt to be unsafe for a resident to attend a particular event, they should be discouraged from taking part.

Residents who are not fully physically and mentally fit may be at risk with regard to health and safety – both theirs and that of others. This will always be a delicate issue, and it will probably be difficult to get the right balance between safeguarding health and safety and negotiating their rights. Where possible, discussions should be held between the resident, the resident's next of kin or other relative(s) and the home manager about what is or is not an acceptable risk. The discussions and any decisions made should be recorded on the resident's notes.

The 'bottom line' will be whether you have done everything that you could reasonably be expected to do to assess and control any risks to the residents.

VEHICLES

Another consideration that may be relevant to your home is the transportation of residents, which may involve your own minibuses or the use of volunteers and their vehicles. This is a complicated area with many responsibilities, particularly on the driver, who is responsible for virtually all aspects of passenger safety on the journey. This mean giving attention, where appropriate, to safety belts, the correct clamping of wheelchairs and vehicle safety.

If this issue is relevant to your home, you may wish to develop and implement a 'vehicle policy' that defines standards for drivers (driving abilities, licence penalties/convictions, health checks), assessing the suitability of residents to go on outings and equipment/vehicle maintenance.

It is important for the driver to fully understand the responsibilities associated with driving residents, and there are training courses run by the Community Transport Association (CTA) for this purpose. You may also require your designated drivers to have periodic health checks to confirm their continued fitness to drive. The frequency of these checks will depend on their age and health status.

Drivers should not be responsible for the care of residents during a journey, so they must be accompanied by an adequate number of carers for the level of care required.

The vehicles should be checked regularly to ensure their safety and roadworthiness. Particular attention should be paid to brakes, tyres and lights. Tail-gate lifts, if present, must be regularly serviced, and have a hand-operated mechanism in addition to any automatic system. Tracking systems for securing wheelchairs must be correctly fitted and kept clean. There must be a secure storage area for keeping items such as straps and clamps not in use: they should not be left loose, because they might become missiles in the event of an accident. The vehicle should also carry a fire extinguisher (dry powder) and a first aid kit.

Other points to think about include providing a mobile phone, ensuring that the vehicles are covered by a 'rescue' service agreement (eg AA or RAC) and never leaving the engine running or the keys in the vehicle when the driver is absent.

When volunteers use their own vehicles for your business, you need – in addition to confirming their fitness and ability to drive, vehicle safety and suitability – to ensure that they have appropriate insurance cover. You may decide that residents should *not* be transported in private vehicles.

In addition to a range of training programmes, the CTA also offer a free advice helpline to their members. Their address is given on page 176.

VIOLENCE

In the previous chapter the risk of violence to staff from the residents was discussed. This chapter looks at the converse situation where the residents are at risk of violence from the staff. As before, violence includes threats, abuse and assault, both mental and physical.

It is quite likely that incidents of violence or abuse will not be reported directly by the victims or other members of staff. This may be because of fear of reprisal or simply because the victim is unable to report such incidents. It will therefore be up to you and your monitoring system to identify these situations so that appropriate action can be taken.

As with all risks, prevention is better than cure so the selection and vetting of all potential members of staff are very important, especially where the residents are particularly vulnerable such as the very old or the infirm.

It is important that all signs of abuse of a resident are investigated to find the cause. Physical signs of violence are obviously easiest to detect, but are probably the rarest form of abuse. Changes in behaviour and signs of uneasiness or restlessness, especially in the presence of the offender (who may be staff or family or visitors), may be indicators of a problem. Staff training in detecting these signs and in dealing with the aftermath is very important.

If a member of staff is found to be committing acts of violence, there should be appropriate disciplinary procedures for dealing with them, based on current employment law practice on gross misconduct. There may also be grounds for criminal proceedings to be taken against the offender – whether a member of staff or a relative or visitor.

CONTRACTORS

The presence of contractors on your premises will almost certainly cause some disruption to normal routines: if not managed properly from the start, it can significantly increase the health and safety risks to your staff and residents.

Contracts

Any contract you draw up with a contractor should deal with health and safety, both in the way the work is to be done and in the standards you expect from any products; for example, work equipment should comply with the rules in the Provision and Use of Work Equipment Regulations 1992 (see Chapter 5). Contracts should also state exactly who is to be responsible for what: for example, who is to provide the equipment and materials, and whether these are to be kept on-site or removed daily. To some extent the type of work involved will decide many of these issues.

The standards of health and safety that you demand from the contractor should be included in the contract terms and conditions.

Co-ordination and co-operation

It is good practice to ask for a copy of the contractor's health and safety policy: this will give a good indication of how they rate the importance of health and safety. (Remember that such policies are required only when five or more people are employed, so small firms may not have a written policy.) Likewise, it may be useful to look at their risk assessment, especially for the work on your premises (again, only employers with five or more employees have to record the significant findings).

A contractor may well ask for a copy of your health and safety policy to familiarise themselves with your emergency procedures and to find out if there are any specific hazards they should be aware of. Even if they do not ask, you can provide one because it indicates the standards of health and safety expected, and gives the contractor an idea of any unavoidable risks that are present. Where special risks are present the contractor should be told about them and any precautions that need to be taken.

Communication at all times is very important and it is good practice to appoint someone on each side to keep regular contact between the parties. From the home's point of view, the manager or someone in authority should be the contact person.

Equipment should not be shared with the contractor, who is responsible for providing workers with the necessary tools and equipment. Contractors should have their own first aid provision, and should inform you about the arrangements. It is possible for you to agree to provide them with first aid but the agreement should be made in writing. (First aid is discussed in Chapter 8.)

YOUNG PEOPLE AND TRAINEES

Young people

Modern health and safety law requires a workplace and systems that are safe and healthy for everyone regardless of their age or gender.

Whilst this is true generally, there are a couple of points worth noting. The duty under section 2 of HASAWA (to ensure the health and safety of employees at work, so far as is reasonably practicable: see Chapter 2) means that employers have a greater responsibility for young people or inexperienced people who may not be familiar with, or perceive dangers associated with, the work. These people therefore need a higher level of supervision until they reach a certain level of competence. Some legislation places prohibitions on certain work (eg involving lead) that cannot be undertaken by young people, although this tends to relate to factories rather than care homes.

The generally accepted definition of a young person is someone between school leaving age and 18 years of age.

The Health and Safety (Young Persons) Regulations 1996 are expected to come into force in the latter part of 1996. They will require a risk assessment to be carried out of the risks to young people before a young person starts their employment. The employment of young people may be prohibited if there is likely to be exposure to specified harmful substances or conditions, but this latter point will not apply to young people on a vocational training programme. (These requirements are based on the HSC's consultative document and *may* change in the final Regulations depending on the responses to the consultation process (completing mid 1996).)

Trainees

Under the Health and Safety (Training for Employment) Regulations 1990, people who are on work experience or government training schemes, and students on 'sandwich' courses, are treated as employees for the purposes of health and safety. They are therefore entitled to the full protection offered by health and safety law. The employer is deemed to be the person providing the training.

- Section 3 of HASAWA requires employers to ensure the health and safety of non-employees who may be harmed by the work.

- General precautions and control measures introduced to reduce risks to staff will also be effective to a certain extent in reducing risks to residents and others.

- Procedures for ensuring that work equipment and substances are securely put away when not in use will further reduce risks; so will ensuring that spillages are cleared up immediately, that obstacles are not left lying about and that there is a good level of lighting, especially where there are changes in floor level.

- Other hazards that need to be dealt with include the temperatures of baths and hot water outlet points, hot surfaces such as radiators, the administration of medicines, activities outside the home, vehicles and violence towards residents by members of staff.

- Contractors can pose special problems from a health and safety point of view; it is important that health and safety is dealt with in the contract. Swopping of health and safety policies between the home and contractor is good practice.

- When contractors are on the premises, there should be defined responsibilities and regular contact between the owner/manager and the contractor. Communication, co-ordination and co-operation are very important. Relevant information, instruction and, if necessary, training should be provided.

- A greater duty of care is owed to people who are young or inexperienced, and who therefore are not familiar with dangers associated with the work.

- Trainees are treated as employees for the purposes of health and safety law.

Relevant guidance

HS(G)104 *Health and safety in residential care homes*

HS(G)155 *Slips and trips*

Available from HSE Books (see p 176).

13 Fire safety

Fire is a serious hazard in all workplaces and requires strict control. In care homes fire may be a particular risk where the residents have some form of physical or mental impairment.

This chapter looks at the main causes of fire and how it spreads through a building, fire prevention, evacuation drills, fire extinguishers and fire risk assessment. Fire policies and fire management are discussed briefly.

LEGISLATION

Building Regulations 1991

There is a close association between the Fire Precautions Act 1971 and the Building Regulations 1991 in connection with standards of fire precautions. The Building Regulations require adequate means of escape and the use of fire-resisting materials in all the buildings to which they apply.

Where the means of escape were constructed in accordance with the Building Regulations, the fire authority can insist on additional structural work only if the means of escape are considered inadequate or the work is necessary to comply with the 1971 Act. Even then the Fire Authority must consult the local authority before insisting on any alterations being made.

Fire Precautions Act 1971

The main legal rules about fire safety are set out in the Fire Precautions Act 1971 (as amended by the Fire Safety and Safety of Places of Sport Act 1987); among other things, this sets up a scheme of fire certificates in designated premises.

Care homes do not need to have a fire certificate, but the Nursing Homes and Mental Nursing Homes Regulations 1984 and the Residential Care Homes Regulations 1984 contain precise fire precaution rules, including:

- adequate means of escape;
- ways to detect, contain and extinguish fires;
- ways to give warnings;
- ways to evacuate everybody from the home;
- maintenance of fire-fighting equipment;
- training staff (and, if possible, residents) on what to do if there is a fire;
- record keeping for:
  - fire practices and drills,
  - fire alarm tests, any defects and the remedial action,
  - what to do if there is a fire.

The registered person – the manager or owner – must consult the registration and inspection unit, building control and fire authority about fire precautions in the home.

Enforcement

The Fire Precautions Act 1971 is enforced by local fire authority inspectors; they have the power of entry to inspect premises that are affected by the Fire Precautions Act 1971 (ie certificated, non-certificated and exempt premises). It is an offence to obstruct fire inspectors in the course of their work or to fail to comply with any conditions they impose.

Improvement and prohibition notices

Fire authorities may issue an 'improvement notice' to occupiers of exempt premises where the required fire precaution standards are not considered satisfactory and there is a risk of fire. The improvement notice will state what work must be done for the premises to comply with the 1971

Act. The occupier may appeal (to the magistrates' court) against the notice within 21 days of receiving it; if there is an appeal, the notice will be suspended until the appeal is decided.

A 'prohibition notice' may be issued by the fire authority where there is a serious risk of fire in any certificated, non-certificated or exempt premises. The prohibition notice will ban or restrict the use of the premises and will take effect immediately if there is a serious risk of personal injury. The occupier may appeal (to the magistrates' court) within 21 days, but the prohibition notice remains in effect and is not suspended until the Court so decides.

Offences

Offences relevant to care homes are:

- Failing to comply with any requirements imposed by the fire authority in connection with proposed alterations.
- Disobeying Regulations made under the 1971 Act.
- Disobeying a prohibition or improvement notice.
- Providing false information.

The defence of 'due diligence' (reasonable care) is set out in the 1971 Act: it is a defence that the occupier took all reasonable precautions and exercised all due diligence to avoid committing an offence.

Changes and alterations

The premises occupier must inform the local registration and inspection authority and the fire authority of any intended changes in the use of the premises or of any structural alterations. The registration and inspection unit, building control and fire authority may inspect the premises to decide the significance of the changes.

The changes and alterations that must be notified include:

- extension or structural alterations;
- reorganisation of internal arrangements (eg furniture, equipment, workplace design and layout);

- keeping the permitted quantities and types of dangerous substances (where dangerous substances were not previously kept);
- changes to the numbers of workers or visitors to the premises.

The ultimate authority is the registration and inspection unit who, having taken advice on fire precautions from the fire service, building control and others, may choose to withdraw the registration of your home. This would mean the closure of the home until the standards set were met.

NOTE The forthcoming Fire Precautions (Places of Work) Regulations will require, among other things, fire risk assessments to be carried out.

COMMON CAUSES OF FIRE

Electrical equipment

The incorrect use and poor maintenance of electrical equipment and appliances are well recognised causes of fires. Precautions that should be taken with electricity are discussed in Chapter 10 (see p 92). Relevant precautions include making sure that:

- all extension leads are fully unwound before use;
- all combustible materials are kept away from any ignition source (eg light bulbs – which can become very hot);
- electric equipment is fitted with the correctly rated fuse, according to the manufacturers' instructions;
- use of overloaded sockets or multiple adaptors.

Smoking

Careless disposal of cigarettes, cigars or pipe tobacco is another common cause of fires. Prevention procedures include:

- using non-combustible and regularly emptied ashtrays and containers;
- prohibiting smoking in high-risk or infrequently used areas;
- prohibiting smoking during the last 30 minutes of the working day; this is usually part of an active smoking policy.

Control over residents' smoking is more difficult and there should be clear policies on where and when smoking is and is not allowed. Any other restrictions must be clearly stated.

Accumulation of refuse

All refuse should be placed in suitable containers that are regularly collected and emptied. Good housekeeping is essential not only in controlling refuse accumulation and disposal but also in ensuring that only the necessary items and quantities of stock are kept on the premises at any time. A build up of refuse encourages arson.

Portable heaters

Carelessly used or poorly controlled portable heaters are other known causes of fires. Their issue and use should be restricted where possible and procedures set up to ensure they are safely positioned while in use and always turned off after use. This can be important where old or infirm people are involved, especially if portable heaters are used in individual rooms.

Fat fryers

The ignition of hot fat is a well known hazard: fat fryers should be fitted with thermostats to control the fat temperature, and they should not be left unattended while in use. A fire blanket should be installed nearby.

Gas and liquefied petroleum gas (LPG)

Where gas can be smelt, no naked lights should be used and no electrical sockets or appliances turned on or off (because sparking inside the appliance or socket may ignite the gas). The gas source must be turned off if possible and the affected area evacuated and ventilated. Such incidents should be reported immediately to the responsible person on duty so that further action, such as informing the Gas Board, can be taken. The Gas Board should be informed immediately if there is a known or suspected gas leak. Explosions resulting from gas leaks must be reported to the enforcing authority under RIDDOR.

Transportable gas containers (eg those containing oxygen or LPG – butane and/or propane) are also recognised fire hazards: the manufacturers' instructions for storage and use must be carefully followed. The Home Office guidance on the use and storage of LPG in residential homes recommends that quantities be restricted to a maximum of 15kg.

Arson

Unfortunately, arson is one of the most common causes of fire, occurring frequently in hospitals and schools. Ways of preventing arson attacks include:

- high standards of premises security;
- regular checks for suspicious objects;
- restricted access to flammable materials and high-risk areas;
- frequent removal of refuse.

Flammable materials

The fire risks associated with flammable materials are obvious and only the minimum amounts necessary should be kept on the premises. The correct storage instructions must be followed; they will include having a secure, properly constructed and designated storage area away from the main building(s). The labels and accompanying data sheets must be read to see if the various substances can be safely stored together.

Contractors

Although not necessarily a cause of fires, the presence of contractors on site can increase the likelihood of fire. It may be useful to give all contractors a copy of the home's fire precautions and evacuation procedures and ensure that they are obeyed. Regular checks should be made on the use and storage of flammable materials used by the contractors. All LPG and other highly flammable material should be removed by the contractor at the end of the working day.

Emergency access

An important part of your fire safety management system will be making sure that both sides of all fire exits are kept clear. It is no use keeping the inside clear if there is a parked car or stack of boxes or some other obstruction on the outside.

Likewise, it is important for emergency vehicles to have unrestricted access to and parking in all areas on-site at all times. This may mean ensuring that gates and/or barriers are staffed, to allow emergency vehicles access in the event of a fire alarm being raised.

FIRE DEVELOPMENT

Fires need three things in order to burn – **heat, fuel** and **oxygen**. These three factors form the fire triangle:

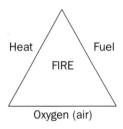

A fire cannot exist if any of these factors is removed: this fact forms the basis on which fires are extinguished. Removal of the oxygen/air (smothering) or of the heat source (cooling) are the main ways in which fire extinguishers work.

SPREAD OF FIRE AND SMOKE

The initial stage of a fire may last a few minutes (flammable material) or several hours (less flammable material); it all depends on the flammability of the materials ignited. Once past this initial stage, fire usually develops rapidly. This emphasises the importance of early detection.

Once a fire has taken hold, there are three ways in which it can spread through a building:

- by convection – the transfer of heat in hot air currents;
- by conduction – the direct transfer of heat between materials;
- by radiation – the transfer of heat as electromagnetic waves.

In most fires a combination of all three heat transfer methods will occur.

Smoke is formed by the mixing of the fumes given off as materials burn and the air present in the area, and usually travels ahead of the fire because of pressure differences formed by the fire. Toxic fumes in some smoke can kill in moments.

Smoke causes adverse physical (watery eyes, restricted ability to breathe) and chemical (toxic fumes) effects, and often results in disorientation and panic because escape routes are obscured. Crawling along at floor level helps people move around and escape from smoke-filled areas.

Compartmentation

'Compartmentation' means the separation of areas from each other in order to delay or stop the spread of any fire that starts. It is an important part of fire protection and of minimising the spread of fire and smoke.

The best time for considering compartmentation is at the planning stage, because it involves the entire building – roof voids and cellars as well as means of escape.

FIRE CLASSIFICATION

Fires are divided into four classes, according to the combustible materials involved. The classification is important when deciding which type of fire extinguisher should be used.

The three classes relevant to care homes are:

Class A Fires involving solid materials (usually organic) such as wood, paper, textiles. The formation of glowing embers usually occurs on combustion.
Extinguisher method: cooling by water.

Class B Fires involving liquids or liquefiable solids (eg petrol, grease, oil, fat).

Extinguisher method: smothering to exclude oxygen.

Class C Fires involving gases (eg hydrogen, propane, butane).

Extinguisher method: cut off source of gas if possible and leave the fire to the experts because of the risk of re-ignition and explosion.

There is no such thing as an electrical fire; this is simply a fire in one of the categories above, in which electricity is also present. Where possible, the electrical supply should be turned off and the appropriate extinguisher chosen for the actual fire. In most cases, carbon dioxide (CO_2) extinguishers will be most appropriate.

Because of the conductivity of water, water extinguishers must *not* be used if electricity is (or is suspected of being) present.

FIRE PROTECTION MEASURES

Fire protection measures can be either 'active' or 'passive'.

Active measures

Active measures are present in the building(s) but will operate only when a fire occurs; these include:

- alarm, extinguishing and automatic detection systems;
- emergency lighting and emergency procedures;
- staff training;
- fire notices and signs;
- systems and route maintenance.

Passive measures

Passive measures are associated with the building design, organisation and use; they include:

- fire-resistant building compartmentation;
- escape and exit routes;

- flame-resistant surfaces and fire-resistant structures and materials;
- building separation.

These measures should be considered in the building planning stages whenever possible.

Evacuation routines

Fire drill training for day staff is recommended once every six months or at the very least annually. This is increased to once every three months for night staff. At least some of the drills should involve the residents so that they are familiar with the evacuation routine.

The training should be more comprehensive than just getting people out of the building, and should also deal with:

- recognition of the fire alarm;
- evacuation procedures;
- knowledge of escape routes;
- procedures for helping disabled people and visitors;
- the importance of establishing whether (or not) everyone is out of the building;
- the dangers of re-entering the building unless told by the emergency services that it is safe to do so.

On discovering a fire

- Raise the alarm immediately by using the nearest manual call point.
- Tackle the fire if it is small, containable and likely to be easily extinguished, but *always* call for assistance. This point will depend on your home's fire policy and whether you want staff to tackle small fires or just evacuate the building. If staff are expected to tackle fires, they must be specifically authorised and fully trained to do so.
- Leave the building immediately if the fire is large, out of control or threatens any escape route – assist residents and visitors where possible.
- Where it is safe to do so, shut doors and windows so as to contain the fire.
- Do not stop, or go back, for personal belongings.
- Report to the Assembly Point.

On hearing the fire alarm

- Leave the building immediately by the nearest available route.
- Assist residents and visitors, and shut doors/windows where it is safe to do so.
- Report to the Assembly Point.

Calling the fire brigade

A designated person should be responsible for calling the fire brigade if there is no direct communication system from the premises to the fire station (but see also p 145). All staff should know:

- when to call the fire brigade;
- the information that needs to be provided (including confirming the details when they are repeated back by the fire brigade); the information given should include:
  - premises details (name, address, etc – which can be kept on a card by the telephone),
  - details of missing people (if any);
- location and type of fire;
- location and involvement of any dangerous materials.

Escape routes

The Building Regulations 1991 contain many rules about optimum escape routes. Protected escape routes are routes that offer a pre-determined degree of fire resistance (usually 30 minutes) and are separated from the rest of the building. They should be provided as an integral part of any building to ensure a satisfactory means of escape. Ideally, it should be possible for people to turn away from a fire and move to a place of safety. Dead-end routes must be avoided, and lifts and escalators should not usually form part of any escape route. Fire escape routes must be kept clear and unobstructed at all times.

Protected corridors must be provided on escape routes in premises used for residential purposes.

Where there are disabled people, escape routes may need to include safe waiting spaces (refuges) such as protected lobbies. The adaptations could include 'tactile' signs, such as braille on handrails, colour contrasts for different areas and different levels of the building or the provision of strategically located collapsible wheelchairs that can quickly be brought into use to help evacuate people with impaired mobility.

Designated lifts may be used in evacuating disabled people but it is recognised that stairways are a more effective and safer means of escape. The use of wheelchair lifts should be avoided where possible.

A single fire should not be able to make *all* escape routes inoperable – there should *always* be an alternative safe route available.

Stairways

Escape stairways should be wide enough to allow the safe evacuation of the maximum number of people expected to be on the premises. This is true even in situations where phased evacuation is practised. Specially designed stairways may also need to be provided to help in the evacuation of disabled people.

Fire doors

Fire doors are provided to prevent the movement of smoke and fire, and to protect the means of escape. All designated fire doors should be fitted with smoke seals that can withstand all smoke at normal temperatures and limited smoke at medium temperatures. They should also be fire resistant for 30 minutes.

Fire doors must be easy to open, and not secured by a lock, latch, bolt or any fastening requiring a key or which requires the operation of more than one mechanism in order to be opened.

Under no circumstances should fire doors be wedged open; where possible, self-closing doors should be fitted. The only exceptions are fire doors held open by automatic release units which release the doors so that they close automatically when the fire alarm system is activated. These should be closed at night. These devices must be tested at least once a week to ensure that they close effectively.

Fire doors should be marked 'FIRE DOOR – KEEP CLOSED' in white letters on a blue background.

Fire exit doors

These must be kept closed and unobstructed at all times (including making sure that they are not obstructed outside by, for example, parked cars or delivery vans), and must open in the direction of the escape. When open, the doors themselves must not obstruct the escape route and they must open to at least 90 degrees. They may be secured but must be readily openable from the inside – this is usually by the use of 'push bar' mechanisms on the door. Other types of locks may be used if there is a risk of residents leaving the building; they are connected to the fire alarm.

Fire exits should be clearly marked in white figures on a green background and, if necessary, illuminated. If the location of the fire exit is not immediately obvious, signs indicating the direction of a fire exit (white symbols and a direction arrow on a green background) should be provided in clearly visible positions.

Fire exits must not be narrower than the escape route and must be sited to allow the maximum evacuation of people to a place of safety away from the building.

Automatic detection systems and fire alarms

Fire warning systems are designed to prevent, or at least minimise, injuries to people and/or losses and damage to property if there is a fire.

In basic terms, a fire warning system will consist of a detector and an alarm system (ie manual call points – break glass units) connected to a central control panel. When a fire occurs, the control panel should be able to identify which zone detector and/or manual call point activated the warning so as to give an indication of the fire's location. In some specialised cases the warning system may be connected to a fixed extinguishing system for automatic operation when the warning system operates.

Building services, such as air conditioning systems and lifts, may also be connected to fire warning systems. There may be a direct communication link between the warning system and the call for the fire brigade – usually through a clearing station that monitors the calls.

Regular maintenance, servicing and testing of fire warning systems is very important.

Automatic detection systems

These rely on one of three characteristics associated with fire: heat, smoke or flames. The advantages of one system over another depend on the specific circumstances, and professional advice should be sought to ensure that the most suitable type is selected.

Fire alarms

The alarm, regardless of the type of sound it emits, must be clear and distinctive, and audible throughout all areas of the building. The minimum level in any part of the premises should be 65dB(A) or a least 5dB(A) above any ambient noise.

In some cases, audible alarms may need to be backed up by visual warning alarms, such as flashing white strobe lights. These should be considered for areas where there are people with reduced hearing abilities or where there is a high level of background noise.

In premises used for sleeping, the required alarm audibility at the bed head is 75dB(A). 'Vibrating alarms' placed under the pillow and connected to the main alarm circuit may be considered necessary for hearing-impaired people, although a variable tone and frequency alarm will often suffice.

A fire alarm should be able to be activated automatically by the detector systems and also manually at the manual call points. It is possible to vary the way in which alarms are sounded in different parts of the premises. For example, all alarms throughout the premises can be sounded (simple alarms), or alarms can be sounded in the area where the alarm was raised and neighbouring areas (zoned alarms), or an evacuation signal can be sounded in the area containing the fire, while the rest of the premises is given an alert signal (two-phase alarm). Most care homes will find that one alarm clearly signalling 'fire' and the need to evacuate is sufficient.

As with all systems, regular maintenance, servicing and testing are essential to ensure that they are in working order. A weekly test of the fire alarm operation is recommended. Fire detectors should be tested every six months; a specialist contractor will be needed for this.

False alarms

It is important to find out the precise cause and extent of any false alarm as soon as possible. This is particularly true if the false alarm results in a reduced level of fire protection (see below). Common causes of false alarms include:

- mechanical and electrical faults in the system (often caused or aggravated by impact, corrosion or vibration);
- environmental factors (eg dust, cigarette smoke, heat, insects in the detector);
- inadequate maintenance or servicing;
- internal changes to the building (eg dust from contract work);
- accidental or malicious operation of manual call points or detectors.

Emergency lighting

Adequate levels of lighting – whether natural or artificial – are essential for the rapid and safe evacuation of buildings.

When the main electrical supply fails, or at night (in areas usually lit by natural light), emergency lighting must give adequate visibility for escape. This applies to localised circuit failure as well as total power failures, if the failure represents a hazard.

Types of emergency lighting

Emergency lights (luminaires) are classified by their power source, and will be one of the following:

- luminaires powered from their own batteries;
- luminaires powered from a central battery system;
- luminaires powered from an electrical generator.

The first group are called 'self-contained luminaires' (ie the battery is part of the luminaire or is situated within one metre of it); the other two groups are called 'slave luminaires'.

In addition, luminaires may be 'maintained' (the luminaires are lit all the time) or 'non-maintained' (they come on when the main power supply fails).

Regular maintenance, servicing and testing of emergency lighting systems is important. A full test of the emergency battery capacity must be made once a year. The whole electrical system must be tested every six months.

FIRE-FIGHTING EQUIPMENT

Fire extinguishers work by removing one or more elements in the fire triangle.

Fixed fire-extinguishing equipment

Fire protection in your premises may be improved by using fixed fire-extinguishing systems, in addition to portable extinguishers and other fire-prevention systems.

There are several types of fixed extinguishing systems; all of them use one of the extinguishing agents found in portable extinguishers. Generally, fixed extinguishing systems operate automatically if there is a fire, or they may be connected to the detection and alarm systems. In some cases there is a short delay so as to allow the safe evacuation of people before the extinguishing system starts to operate.

The fire extinguishers available include water sprinklers, foam, carbon dioxide (CO_2) and dry powder. Professional advice should be sought on their selection, positioning and use.

As with all systems concerned with fire protection and prevention, the regular maintenance, servicing and testing of fixed extinguishing systems is very important in ensuring their continued effectiveness. All fire extinguishers must be inspected by a competent person once every fourteen months. A specialist contractor should be appointed for these inspections.

Reduced protection situations

If the normal level of fire protection is reduced for any reason (eg during maintenance), the following steps should be taken so as to give the best level of protection in the circumstances:

- Inform the insurance company and fire brigade immediately so that they can advise on appropriate action.
- Introduce (and insist on) a total smoking ban in the affected areas.
- Ensure that there are adequate portable extinguishers available for *immediate* use.
- Arrange *continual* surveillance of the area.
- Stop hazardous activities in the area for the period of reduced protection.
- Ensure that the systems work properly when restored.
- Inform the insurance company and fire brigade when full protection has been restored.

PORTABLE FIRE EXTINGUISHERS

There are several types of extinguishing medium available which are more or less effective against the different classes of fire (see p 139). It is therefore very important that staff know these differences because using the wrong extinguisher on a fire can make the situation a lot worse.

The fire extinguishers are all colour coded according to the extinguishing medium they use. The colour usually covers the entire body of the extinguisher, but some extinguishers are just plain chrome or red with the appropriate colour coding in a prominent place on the body. The following table summarises the different extinguishers, the colour code and the way they work.

Extinguisher	Colour	Extinguishing method	For use on
Water	Red	Cooling (removes heat)	Class A fires DO NOT USE ON LIVE ELECTRICAL EQUIPMENT OR BURNING LIQUIDS
Foam	Cream	Smothering (excludes oxygen)	Class B fires DO NOT USE ON LIVE ELECTRICAL EQUIPMENT
Carbon dioxide (CO_2)	Black	Smothering (excludes oxygen)	Class B fires DO NOT USE IN CONFINED SPACES; DO NOT TOUCH THE NOZZLE BECAUSE THE CO_2 CAN CAUSE FREEZE BURNS
Dry powder	Blue	Knocks down flames	Class A and B fires
Halon*	Green	Knocks down flames	Class B fires and *small* class A fires DO NOT USE IN CONFINED SPACES: THERE MAY BE TOXIC FUMES
Hose reel	Red	Cooling (removes heat)	Class A fires DO NOT USE ON LIVE ELECTRICAL EQUIPMENT
Fire blanket	Red	Smothering (excludes oxygen)	Class A and B fires

* Halon has been discontinued as a fire-extinguishing medium, under the Montreal Protocol for maintaining the ozone layer. Once existing units have passed their shelf life they will not be replaced by new halon extinguishers.

Each extinguisher has printed on its body clear instructions for use.

STAFF TRAINING

Responsible persons

Staff need to be clear what their specific responsibilities are if there is a fire. Exactly how these responsibilities are decided will depend on the particular organisation, but the following 'designated' personnel may be considered. This does not remove the need for all staff to receive basic fire training but the training required will vary with – and should take account of – the responsibilities taken on. Someone, usually the proprietor or a senior manager in the home, with enough authority to 'mobilise' people and finances, should be responsible for developing, implementing, monitoring and reviewing or revising the fire policy, including staff training programmes.

All staff

Owing to the flexible nature of staffing in care homes, it may not be possible to give specific duties to individual staff. Therefore, all staff must be trained to respond to a fire or fire alarm. Frequent practice will help confirm these responses and duties. Staff should be trained to identify if they are in the area where the fire is; if so, they should start evacuating all people in that area. Other staff should be trained to identify the fire area, approach it with care and control, and then assist with the evacuation to a place of safety. The place of safety is usually defined as at least two *closed* fire doors away from the seat of the fire or outside to open air. Staff must feel confident to telephone the fire brigade without any reference to other or senior staff. The staffing levels in a care home may not be sufficient for a total evacuation of the building, especially where there are infirm residents. Only by calling the fire brigade immediately will help be obtained. Staff should be trained to carry out a 'first phase' evacuation as quickly as possible while the fire brigade is on its way. This first phase should start in the areas closest to the fire and be accomplished in about two to three minutes. The fire brigade should arrive in five to twelve minutes.

These staff will be responsible for shutting down plant, machinery and systems (eg air conditioning systems) that can spread fire and smoke.

FIRE RISK ASSESSMENT

The principles of fire risk assessment are the same as for general health and safety risk assessments:

- identification of hazards;
- evaluation of risks;
- determination of suitable and effective measures to control the risks.

To understand fire risk assessment, it is important to know the difference between fire hazard and fire risk.

- **Fire hazard** is the *potential* something has to cause a fire.
- **Fire risk** is the *likelihood* of the fire hazard occurring and the *extent and severity* of the damage.

The fire risk assessment should form the starting point of your fire policy – which in turn should be a basic part of your overall health and safety management system.

Hazard identification

This is the first stage of the risk assessment and should include all significant hazards. Hazard identification will require consideration of all situations that may result in fire and should take into account:

- work areas
- work procedures
- work processes and activities
- equipment
- materials (raw materials, end products and waste)
- personnel

The building itself may also be labelled as a high, medium or low risk by the fire authority. The risk level is decided by applying certain criteria.

A building will be labelled **high** risk where:

- sleeping accommodation is provided;
- flammable materials are present;

- undesirable building structures exist (in this situation the registration and inspection unit would withdraw registration of the home);
- high-risk activities or processes are carried out;
- there are many staff and/or residents and/or visitors.

Care homes are likely to fall into this high-risk category.

A building will be labelled **medium** risk where:

- a fire will remain localised and spread only very slowly;
- the contents, structures, processes etc are unlikely to represent a significant fire hazard;
- the number of people likely to be affected is small.

This category includes most workplaces.

A building will be labelled **low** risk where:

- there is very little flammable material;
- the risk of fire and smoke spreading is minimal.

In practice, very few premises fall into this category.

Risk evaluation

After identifying all the significant fire hazards, the risk evaluation will determine how likely the fire hazard is to occur and what the likely damage to people and property will be. Remember that the situation may vary, such as when contractors are working in the building.

The risk evaluation should take into account:

- the building risk category;
- the work being carried out;
- the materials and equipment involved;
- the people involved;
- the means of escape;
- structural compartmentations and the possible spread of fire and smoke;
- fire warning measures;
- maintenance, service and repair procedures.

For each hazard and the factors linked to it you should ask if:

- the risk is negligible;
- the risk is acceptable;
- safe working practices are in place;
- effective control measures exist;
- the risk is outside your control (eg in someone else's control, such as a contractor).

Your judgement on all these questions is arbitrary and depends on the particular circumstances. There are no standard right or wrong answers.

Because risk evaluation consists of 'likelihood' and 'extent/severity' factors, the following definitions may be helpful. The *likelihood* will be:

- **high** if a fire will certainly, or almost certainly, occur from the fire hazard;
- **medium** if a fire could occasionally occur from the fire hazard;
- **low** if a fire is unlikely to occur from the fire hazard.

The *extent/severity* rating will be:

- **high** if it is likely or very likely that damage will occur;
- **medium** if it is possible that some damage could occur;
- **low** if it is unlikely that any damage will occur.

Remembering that Risk = Likelihood × Extent/Severity, numerical values can be used for the three likelihood and the three extent/severity groups; they can then be multiplied together to give a 'risk value'. For example, treating high as 3, medium as 2 and low as 1, a situation with a high likelihood and high extent/severity rating would give a risk value of $3 \times 3 = 9$. A low likelihood and high extent/severity rating would give a risk of value of $1 \times 3 = 3$. In this way risks can be readily compared, the higher numerical risk values calling for more urgent attention.

Control measures

The control (preventive and protective) measures should deal with the risk evaluations outlined above. Priority should be given to measures that protect the whole workforce and work premises.

The control 'hierarchy' or order when deciding the most effective control measures should be:

- Avoid the fire risk completely whenever possible.

- Flammable materials should be replaced by less flammable ones.
- Where the risks cannot be avoided, they should be controlled at source.
- Use technological improvements to improve fire safety.
- Develop, use, monitor, review and revise safe working practices.
- Relocate or reorganise work so as to reduce fire risks.

An important part of any system of controls is the effective training of all staff in the hazards and necessary controls associated with their work.

FIRE POLICY

The fire policy should be based on the fire risk assessment and should state:

- the organisation's commitment to fire safety;
- the responsibilities of 'designated' personnel and other staff;
- the arrangements for implementing, ensuring and improving safe fire practices.

These requirements are the same as are required in health and safety policies under section 2(3) of HASAWA, and it will be sensible to combine the two into one comprehensive policy.

FIRE SAFETY MANAGEMENT

This should involve commitment from senior management to detail and put into effect a plan for achieving your fire policy. This will include the planning, organisation, control, monitoring and reviewing of the fire risk assessment and associated control measures.

Responsibility for doing the fire risk assessment may be delegated, but senior management remains responsible for ensuring that it is carried out by a competent person. The responsibility for your procedural framework for the guidance, training and – most importantly – resources (in terms of both people and money) in implementing and maintaining the fire policy, and in making sure the law is obeyed, also rests with senior management.

- Fire needs fuel, heat and oxygen (air) in order to burn; removing any one of these elements in the fire triangle will provide a means of extinguishing the fire.

- The most common causes of fire are faulty or misused electrical equipment, smoking, portable heaters, fat fryers, gas and liquefied petroleum gas, and arson.

- Fire protection measures are either 'active' (ie operate when a fire occurs) or 'passive' (ie associated with the building design and structure).

- Active measures include alarm, extinguishing and detection systems; emergency lighting; training; fire notices and signs; and regular, recorded system/equipment maintenance.

- Fire evacuation drills are an important part of fire safety and should be done at least once a year. Residents should be included in some drills.

- Fire escape routes, fire doors and fire exits must never be obstructed, and fire-related doors must be kept shut unless they are held open on magnets and close automatically when the alarm operates.

- Emergency lighting must be provided to deal with a mains power failure.

- Portable fire extinguishers are colour coded according to their extinguishing medium. Not all extinguishers are safe on all fires so it is important for staff authorised to fight fires to know which extinguisher to use.

- Fire risk assessments will be legally required when the Fire Precautions (Places of Work) Regulations come into force. They are very similar to ordinary health and safety risk assessments (outlined in Chapter 1).

- As with health and safety, fire safety must be dealt with as a basic part of the business's management system; it is good practice to develop and implement a fire safety policy, again along the lines of the health and safety policy. The two policies could well be joined to form one comprehensive document.

Relevant guidance

Fire safety management in hotels and boarding houses

Fire Precautions Act 1971: fire safety at work

FIRECODE (these are a series of booklets dealing with fire prevention in the NHS)

All the above are available from HMSO (see p 176).

14 Food safety

Although food safety is not a matter of health and safety as such, some of the main ideas involved are very similar, and many organisations treat them as a combined subject.

This chapter discusses the basic principles of food safety and food hygiene, including the main causes of food poisoning, susceptible groups of people, cross-contamination, personal hygiene, time/temperature controls and training. Other factors such as stock control, pest control, kitchen design and layout, and cleaning routines are also discussed briefly.

LEGISLATION

Food Safety Act 1990

The Food Safety Act 1990 deals with the safety of food throughout the food chain – from the farm to the ultimate consumer. As with HASAWA, subsidiary Regulations can be made by Government departments to lay down more detailed rules when needed.

The Food Safety Act is enforced by environmental health officers (EHOs) or trading standards officers (TSOs), depending on the offence: EHOs enforce the food safety provisions, TSOs the consumer-related provisions such as misleading labelling.

EHOs have powers under the 1990 Act to require improvements to unhygienic premises; in bad cases they may close down premises that pose a serious risk to health. They may also enter food premises at any reasonable time, inspect food, take samples for investigation and take away suspect food.

The main offences under the Act are:

- selling food unfit for human consumption;
- selling food that has been rendered harmful to health;
- rendering food harmful to health;
- selling food that is so contaminated that it is unreasonable to expect it to be eaten;
- selling food that is not of the nature, substance or quality demanded by the public;
- falsely or misleadingly presenting food.

The Act allows the defence of 'due diligence': this means that the person charged with the offence took all reasonable precautions and exercised due diligence to avoid committing it. To be able to demonstrate this, you will have to keep records of temperatures taken at different times and points of the food chain in your home and show that you have carried out some form of food safety risk assessment. You also need to use reputable suppliers, and you are entitled to ask them for evidence of their due diligence. Training of food handlers will also be important (see p 159).

Food Safety (General Food Hygiene) Regulations 1995

The Food Safety (General Food Hygiene) Regulations 1995 deal with the safe preparation and sale of food for human consumption. Unlike previous prescriptive legislation, these Regulations lay down general principles of food hygiene to be achieved; more importantly, an assessment of the risks must be made whenever there is a possibility of the food becoming contaminated. The points most relevant to care homes are discussed below.

Food premises and storage

Food proprietors have specific duties, including meeting all the minimum hygiene standards contained in the Schedule to the Regulations. Premises must be well maintained and clean, and all surfaces must be able to be cleaned and, if necessary, disinfected. There must also be adequate lighting, ventilation, a wholesome drinking water supply, toilets (which must not lead directly to a food area), and adequate and separate facilities for washing hands, food and equipment. There must also be adequate drainage to food areas, effective pest control and facilities for food refuse to be safely stored and disposed of.

Food must be stored in suitable conditions and protected from contamination and deterioration. Food that is contaminated or unfit for human consumption must not be accepted into the premises.

The design, construction and layout of food areas is important and should be considered in the food safety risk assessment. For example, new equipment should be positioned and installed so that it and the area around it can be cleaned easily after installation.

Food handlers

The food proprietor must ensure that food handlers maintain the highest standards of personal hygiene. Any food handler known or suspected of suffering from or carrying a food-transmitted disease which could lead to the food becoming contaminated with pathogenic (disease-causing) bacteria must be suspended from all food-related duties. Food handlers must report any such conditions to the proprietor – this includes situations in which they may be exposed to similar medical conditions within their family or household.

Training

All food handlers must receive food hygiene training appropriate to their food handling duties. This means that everyone involved in any aspect of food preparation, service, washing up and so on must undergo some form of training. The greater the responsibility for ensuring the safety of food, the higher the level of training that is required. For example, a head chef or catering manager would be expected to undertake a much higher level of training than the kitchen porter. Your local environmental health department should be able to advise you on appropriate training courses.

Food safety assessments

A food safety risk assessment must be carried out to identify the stages in which contamination could occur, and to determine the control measures needed to eliminate these risks or at least reduce them to the minimum.

The food safety risk assessment is based on exactly the same principles as the health and safety risk assessment discussed in Chapter 2, and should look at every stage from purchase specifications through to service. The system of *assured safe catering* has been designed specially to help catering businesses to carry out their food safety risk assessments. Relevant guidance is given at the end of the chapter.

Food Safety (Temperature Control) Regulations 1995

These Regulations define the temperatures that must be maintained during various food-related activities.

Cold food

High risk foods – foods that allow harmful bacteria to grow and/or produce toxins (harmful chemicals) – must be kept at 8°C or below when they are held in cold storage.

You may keep food above 8°C, provided it is used within the specified shelf life, where manufacturers have indicated that it is safe to do so, and all relevant temperature and shelf-life information is provided on the label or in other written instructions. There are some exceptions to this requirement, including:

- food that must be kept hot;
- food that may be safely kept at ambient (room) temperature;
- food that has undergone a preservation process such as canning (provided the can has not been opened) or dehydration (provided water has not been added to the food);
- food that is matured or ripened at ambient temperatures (although it may have to comply with the 8°C limit after it has matured or ripened);
- food that will receive further treatment, provided that the further treatment ensures that the food is safe and fit to eat.

Food temperatures may rise above 8°C (or any specified temperature) if you can prove that the food was intended for service, had not previously exceeded 8°C (or any other recommended storage temperature), and had been kept for service or display for less than four hours. A temperature higher than 8°C is accepted when it is unavoidable during processing or preparation or because of equipment failure.

Food must be cooled to the required temperature as quickly as possible after cooking or the final preparation stage – food should be at ambient temperature for the minimum amount of time.

Hot food

Cooked or reheated food that is to be served or sold, and which needs to be kept hot in order to control bacterial growth and toxin formation, must be kept at 63°C or above. A person charged with contravening this requirement may offer in defence proof that the food intended for service, or displayed for sale, had been below 63°C for less than two hours, and had not previously been offered for service or sale. It is also a defence to prove that the food was safe at temperatures below 63°C for a specified period of time, according to well-founded scientific assessments.

General requirements

The Regulations also prohibit any food items being kept at temperatures likely to pose a risk to health, although certain variations from the specified temperatures are allowed if they are necessary during any handling activities.

NOTE It is possible to contravene this general temperature requirement even if the more specific hot or cold temperature requirements *have been* complied with. For example, if the manufacturer recommends that a food be kept at 5°C or below and it is kept at 7°C, this could be a contravention of the general requirement even though the food is below the cold holding temperature of 8°C.

Scottish requirements

In Scotland cold food must be kept in a refrigerator, refrigerated chamber or cool ventilated place; no specific temperature is defined but the requirement of 8°C in England and Wales is good guidance. Hot food must be kept at 63°C or above, as in England and Wales. In addition, reheated food must reach 82°C unless this temperature causes a deterioration in the food quality. The requirements for avoiding holding food at temperatures likely to pose a risk to health (except in the defined circumstances) and the exceptions relating to contraventions of the hot and cold holding requirements are similar to those in England and Wales. Gelatine used for confectionery fillings, meat and/or fish products must either reach 100°C or be held at 71°C for 30 minutes immediately prior to use. Any gelatine not used must be cooled as quickly as possible and, when cold, placed in a refrigerator, refrigerated chamber or cool ventilated place, or disposed of.

Food Premises (Registration) Regulations 1991

These Regulations require all food premises to be registered with their local food authority (usually the local council), so that the authorities can develop strategic inspection procedures based on the type of food business and the degree of risk. There are exceptions to these Regulations but they are unlikely to apply to care homes where food is prepared and served on a regular basis.

FOOD HYGIENE

Food poisoning

Food poisoning is an illness caused by consuming food or drink that has been contaminated. The contamination is usually (but need not be) bacterial; large numbers of bacteria are required to cause the illness but they do multiply in the food. Nowadays, food-borne diseases (eg typhoid, tuberculosis, dysentery) that are transmitted via food are also included in the definition. In these cases only small amounts of bacteria are necessary to cause illness and the bacteria do not have to multiply in the foods.

Susceptible groups

Anyone can suffer from food poisoning – an ailment that can produce symptoms ranging from a vague feeling of stomach ache to severe vomiting, diarrhoea, dehydration and, in extreme cases, neurological disorders and death. The following groups of people are particularly susceptible to food poisoning:

- the very young – babies and small children;
- the very old;
- people who are infirm (eg frail residents);
- pregnant women.

Care homes will almost certainly be providing food for at least one of these groups. Some older residents may also be infirm; this increases the need to observe and enforce good food hygiene practices.

Causes and sources of food poisoning
Causes

Food poisoning may be caused by several different things – bacteria, viruses, chemicals, poisonous plants and metal (eg lead, mercury). Of these, bacteria are by far the most common cause, and only they are considered in the rest of this chapter.

Bacteria are tiny living organisms that live everywhere – in the air, water, soil, and in or on humans and animals. They are invisible to the naked eye and can been seen only with a microscope. Not all are harmful; some are necessary to aid digestion and some are used to make certain types of cheeses and yoghurts. The harmful bacteria are collectively known as pathogens.

Food-poisoning bacteria

The most common food poisoning bacteria are:

- *Salmonella*
- *Staphylococcus aureus*
- *Clostridium perfringens*
- *Campylobacter*
- *Listeria*
- *Bacillus cereus*

Bacteria can cause food poisoning in a number of ways. Some bacteria (eg *Staphylococcus aureus*) produce and release chemical toxins on to the food, causing poisoning when the food is eaten. There is usually a rapid onset of symptoms (which include nausea and vomiting) after eating the contaminated food and a rapid recovery. Foods at risk include cooked foods that will not receive further heat treatment.

Other bacteria cause an infection in the gut which in turn leads to food poisoning (eg *Salmonella* and *Clostridium perfringens*). The onset of symptoms is usually slower and may include vomiting, diarrhoea and abdominal pain. Recovery often takes longer as well. Frail elderly people may not recover at all.

Some bacteria can also form spores: these are hard, very resilient cases formed by the bacteria in order to survive unfavourable living conditions. Once favourable conditions return, the bacteria will regenerate and continue to live and grow normally. Bacterial spores are extremely difficult to kill except at very high temperatures. *Clostridium perfringens* is able to form spores.

Sources of food-poisoning bacteria

The most common sources of food-poisoning bacteria are:

- humans, especially the food handlers;
- raw foods, especially poultry, meats, fish and eggs;
- waste food and refuse;
- pests (eg rats, mice, flies, cockroaches, pets and birds).

The transfer of food-poisoning bacteria from the source to the food is known as 'cross-contamination'.

Food handlers

Food-poisoning bacteria are commonly found in the nose, mouth, throat and gut of humans (and animals) and on the skin and hair. Therefore sneezing, coughing, nose picking, touching hair or areas of skin are all ways of transferring bacteria from the body to the food. Likewise, smoking (which is prohibited by law in food areas) allows contact between fingers and mouth and the subsequent transfer of bacteria. Blowing on food to cool it down is another means of transferring bacteria directly on to the food. Bacteria from the gut may get on to food when food handlers do not wash their hands frequently and especially after using the toilet, or if water contaminated with sewage comes into contact with food.

High standards of personal hygiene are of the greatest importance in preventing contamination directly from food handlers. Some precautions are required by law: for example, covering open and/or septic cuts with waterproof (coloured) dressings, wearing clean overalls to prevent personal clothing contaminating food and reporting certain illnesses. In addition, food handlers must wash their hands:

■ after using the toilet

■ every time they enter a food area

■ after handling raw foods

■ after touching any part of their body or clothing

■ after sneezing, coughing, blowing their nose

■ after smoking

■ after handling refuse

■ after handling chemicals.

NOTE Hands must be washed only in the special wash hand basins, which must be supplied with soap, nailbrushes and a means of drying the hands.

Other problems include preventing food handlers wearing jewellery (except for plain band rings) and providing suitable head-wear to stop hair falling into food. It is also against the law for food handlers to spit in food areas.

Raw foods

Raw food is another common source of food poisoning bacteria, and contamination occurs as a result of failures in hygiene practices. Animals and plants used to produce food for consumption are covered in bacteria; some of these can cause food poisoning, and they will be carried on the raw food into the kitchen and other food areas. It is therefore very important to control what happens to raw food when it is handled and stored.

One of the biggest problem areas is contamination caused by the same utensils, work surfaces or equipment being used for both raw and cooked food preparation. Ideally, there should be separate tools and equipment for raw and for cooked foods. These are now available with colour coding so as to provide a clear indication of their proper use and to minimise errors. For example, chopping boards and knives used for raw meat might be colour coded red, those for fish blue, and those for vegetables green.

If separate items cannot be provided, they must be thoroughly washed after *each* use and left clean for the next time. 'Clean as you go' is a good rule to follow because it reduces the risk of people using dirty items unawares.

Correct storage procedures in refrigerators will also help to reduce the risk of cross-contamination. Cooked foods and foods not receiving further heat treatment should be stored at the top of the refrigerator. Raw foods (especially raw meats) should be put in trays and placed at the bottom, so that they cannot drip on to and contaminate other foods.

Vegetables and fruit may be covered in chemicals such as fertilisers and pesticides, as well as harbouring bacteria from the air or soil. These items should therefore be washed thoroughly in sinks designated for 'food use' only. Some food businesses rinse salad items in a sterilising agent; if you choose to do this, make sure that the agent is safe for food use (eg use one intended for baby bottles). Clean water is usually sufficient to wash salad items.

It is also good practice to try to designate part of the kitchen a food preparation area so as to develop a flow system that prevents, or minimises, raw and cooked foods coming into contact with each other.

Waste food and refuse

Food hygiene law requires suitable lidded refuse containers to be provided in food areas. There should also be suitable, easily cleaned and pest-proof designated areas away from the food areas (eg outside) for keeping refuse containers, and arrangements for the regular collection of refuse so that it does not accumulate and attract pests.

Pests

Common food pests include rodents (rats and mice), birds (pigeons), pets (cats and dogs) and insects (flies, cockroaches, ants). They all naturally harbour or, because of their life habits, carry food-poisoning bacteria. Regular monitoring of all food-related areas is important in detecting early signs of infestation; signs to look out for include:

- droppings;
- damage to boxes, food containers, wall plaster, wood etc, especially from rodents;
- unusual smells;
- spillages next to stored food;
- marks on walls, pipes etc from the fur of rodents;
- small mounds of food.

When a pest problem is noticed, it is good practice to call in a pest control company to assess the extent of the problem and deal with it. Pest control is a specialist business and proper use of the substances employed to kill the pests is very important, as is finding all the dead carcasses so that they do not pose a further health risk.

Pest control experts will also be able to offer advice on pest-proofing your food areas: methods include providing fly-screens over windows, and electronic ultra-violet fly-killers.

Advice on pest control is available from most local authority environmental health departments.

Conditions for bacterial growth

In order to grow, all food-poisoning bacteria need:

- food
- moisture
- warmth
- time

By removing any one of these factors, bacterial growth can be prevented or at least controlled. It is, of course, impossible to remove the food element because the reason it is there is to feed the residents. It is therefore important to realise that some foods are especially high risk in terms of food poisoning.

These high risk foods are the high protein foods which also contain a reasonable amount of moisture (water). Examples are: cooked meat and poultry; dairy products, including artificial cream products; fish and shellfish; gravies and stocks; cooked rice; and eggs and egg products.

NOTE   Food that has been contaminated with food-poisoning bacteria usually looks, smells and tastes completely normal.

It is difficult to remove the moisture factor. Dry foods are a recognised means of preserving food and increasing storage shelf life, but, as soon as the food is reconstituted by adding water, it again becomes a normal perishable food.

This leaves time and temperature as the easier means for controlling bacterial growth, and if managed properly are the most effective control measures available. These are discussed in detail below.

Time and temperature controls

Time

One of the four conditions bacteria need to grow is time, and this, combined with temperature control, provides the most effective means of preventing or minimising bacterial growth.

Given the conditions needed for growth, food-poisoning bacteria can double their numbers every 10–20 minutes. Remember that there will be thousands of bacterial cells present at the beginning, not just one. At a doubling rate of 10–20 minutes, 1000 bacteria can become 1,000,000 in 1 hour 40 minutes.

Time on its own is difficult to control because time is needed to prepare food safely and to serve it.

Temperature

Although the legal requirements on food temperatures are fairly complicated, there is a simple rule that should be followed at all times: 'keep it cool or keep it hot'.

Food-poisoning bacteria have an optimum growth temperature of around 37°C (body temperature) but are capable of reasonable growth rates between 5°C and 63°C. This temperature range is known as the 'danger zone', and food should be kept in this zone for the shortest possible time. Especially at risk are foods left out in warm rooms or foods that have been cooked and are cooling down before going into the refrigerator.

It is not practical to put hot food directly into a refrigerator, because this will raise its operating temperature. Such food should be cooled and refrigerated within 90 minutes from the end of cooking.

Food is vulnerable during this cooling down period, not just because it will be in the 'danger zone' but also because it may be contaminated from other sources. For example, food left to cool by open windows may be contaminated by the air being drawn over it. Such food should be put in the coolest, most sheltered place available, and covered over. Other temperatures to be aware of include:

Temperature (°C)	Activity
below zero	freezers (variable depending on freezer capacity)
1–4	optimum operating temperature of refrigerators
20	bacteria start to grow
37	optimum growth
63	bacteria start to die
70	pasteurisation
75	reheated food and core temperature of cooked foods must achieve this
83	heat disinfection
120+	spores killed

These temperatures are important to remember.

NOTE 1   Freezers and refrigerators should have thermometers in them so that the temperatures can be checked easily. These temperature readings should be recorded along with the date, time and any other relevant details. This will help to demonstrate 'due diligence' (see p 158). Readings should be taken at least daily – preferably first thing in the morning when the unit has been undisturbed/unopened all night.

NOTE 2   Cooked food and prepared food that is reheated must reach at least 75°C in its centre. Food may be reheated only once and then must be disposed of if it is not used. Food probe thermometers for checking food temperatures will be very useful. These temperatures should be taken regularly at different meal times and places, and recorded; it is not necessary to check every item – concentrate on reheated and high risk foods.

Stock control

How food is stored when it arrives at your home and after it has been prepared is an important aspect of food safety. The following is general advice on storage practice and stock control.

- Check all food deliveries to confirm that the contract specifications have been met – look for signs of pest damage (you may be about to let some into your home), check and record the temperature of all cold deliveries, check that the stock is within its 'use by' or 'best before' dates and make a note of the delivery date.
- Freezers work most efficiently when packed tightly with food.
- Refrigerators work most efficiently when the cold air can circulate around the food – they should *not* be packed tightly.
- Check the date codes on all food regularly – throw away any food that has passed its 'use by' or 'best before' dates.
- Operate a stock rotation system for storing food: first in – first out; always put new stock behind old stock so that the oldest food is used first.

Cleaning

Cleaning is another important part of food safety. Generally, all utensils and equipment should be 'cleaned as you go' so that the risk of cross-contamination is reduced.

A lot of washing up is now carried out by mechanical dishwashers, which clean the items with a detergent to remove dirt and grease (the main food debris is removed beforehand) and then subject them to a very hot rinse capable of disinfecting the items. Because the final rinse is so hot the washed items tend to dry very quickly in the air, thus dispensing with the need for drying towels. Maintenance of these machines is important so as to ensure that the correct temperatures are achieved.

Washing up by hand follows a similar system although the water temperatures are much lower for safety reasons. Equipment must be washed up only in sinks designated for that purpose.

Work surfaces should be washed down with sanitiser (a chemical that combines the properties of a detergent to remove grease and fats and a disinfectant that reduces bacterial numbers to safe levels) after each use, as well as before and after work each day. Equipment and utensils should be stored away from possible sources of contamination.

Cleaning also involves the actual food areas such as walls, ceilings and floors. Some organisations call in outside contractors to carry out a 'deep clean' of all food areas at regular intervals. Ducting and extraction hoods and the like must also be cleaned down regularly, not only for food safety reasons but also from a fire hazard point of view. Filters in the extraction system will need to be replaced regularly as well.

KEY POINTS

- Very old and infirm people are particularly susceptible to food poisoning.

- Food poisoning is an illness caused by eating contaminated food. High risk foods include the moist, high protein foods such as cooked meat, dairy products, egg and egg products, fish and shellfish.

- Bacteria are the main cause of food poisoning, but it can also be caused by chemicals, viruses and poisonous plants.

- Bacteria need food, moisture, time and warmth to grow; of these, time and temperature offer the most effective means of controlling bacterial growth.

- The temperature danger zone in which bacteria grow best is between 5°C and 63°C – so keep food either cold (below 5°C) or hot (above 63°C); the optimum temperature for growth is 37°C.

- Freezers should operate at between –18°C and –22°C; refrigerators should operate at between 1°C and 4°C.

- Cooked and reheated foods should reach at least 75°C at their centre.

- Prevent cross-contamination of prepared food from recognised sources of food-poisoning bacteria such as food handlers, raw foods, waste food and refuse, and pests.

- The storage of food and the cleaning routines for equipment and premises are important parts of food hygiene.

Relevant guidance

Hygiene for management by Richard A Sprenger, available from Highfield Publications, Vue Pointe, Spinney Hill, Sprotbrough, Doncaster, South Yorkshire DN5 7LY.

Basic food hygiene certificate coursebook, Chartered Institute of Environmental Health, Chadwick Court, 15 Hatfields, London SE1 8DJ.

Assured safe catering – a management system for hazard analysis, Department of Health, available from HMSO (see p 176).

PB0351 *Food Safety Act 1990 and you – a guide for the food industry* (free).

PB0370 *Food Safety Act 1990 and you – a guide for caterers and their employees* (free).

PB1649 *Keeping food cool and safe* (free).

PB0553 *Understanding food labels* (free).

All the free leaflets listed above are available from Food Sense, London SE99 7TT.

A guide to food hazards and your business – identifying and controlling potential food hazards (free)

A guide to the general food hygiene Regulations (free)

A guide to the general temperature control Regulations (free)

These three are available from the Department of Health, PO Box 410, Wetherby LS23 7LN.

Industry guide to good hygiene practice: catering guide, available from HMSO (see p 176).

Glossary

There are several words and terms used in this book that may need greater clarification. Most of the words in this glossary have legal implications, which are explained. All the words are defined in the context of health and safety only, even if there are other meanings that may be applicable.

Absolute duty This is a term used in law to indicate whether something must or must not be done. It is usually written as 'shall' or 'shall not'. See also 'Practicable' and 'Reasonably practicable'.

Acts These are the primary pieces of law, and usually define general principles or standards to be achieved. Acts (or 'Bills' as they are initially called) are considered by Parliament, who may require changes before they are finally agreed as law. See also 'Regulations'.

Adverse(ly) Something that has the effect of causing a deterioration in an existing standard. In the case of health and safety, this means anything that increases the risk of accidents, ill-health or injuries.

Approved codes of practice (ACOPs) These are documents published by the Health and Safety Commission (HSC) which supplement certain pieces of legislation by providing guidance/information on the legal standards to be achieved. It is not an offence to ignore an approved code of practice provided these standards are achieved by other means. However, if an approved code of practice is ignored and the specified standards are not achieved by other means, the failure to follow the approved code of practice can be used in court as evidence of non-compliance.

Breach of legal duty This means a failure to meet a legal obligation – not doing what the law requires you to do.

Competent person This is generally accepted as someone who has the knowledge, skill, qualifications, training or experience to perform a specific task safely. Except in one or two very specific cases, 'competent person' is not legally defined.

Comply This means fulfilling all your legal obligations.

Contravention This means failing to comply with your legal obligations.

Enforcement notices These are orders which environmental health officers may impose to ensure that the law is complied with. There are two types of enforcement notices: improvement notices and prohibition notices. Both of these are discussed in more detail in Chapter 1.

Guidance notes These are documents published by the HSC/HSE to provide practical and technical information on ways in which the law can be complied with. They tend to be more detailed than approved codes of practice and relate to recommended good practices as opposed to defining legal requirements.

In force This relates to legislation that is current – laws that must be complied with *now*. See also 'Repeal and revoke'.

Legal duty This is something that the law requires you to do (or not to do), as written down in Acts or Regulations.

Legislation This is a general term that is used to mean 'written laws'. It includes 'Acts' and 'Regulations', which are pieces of legislation.

Modified Health and safety is a subject that is constantly changing in the light of technological developments and advances in good practice. This means that in some cases the law must be amended to keep pace with the changes. It is not always feasible to make new legislation, so existing legislation is modified by newer legislation, to incorporate relevant developments. See also 'Repeal and revoke'.

Practicable This is a slightly less strict duty than an *absolute duty* (which see) and requires risks to be controlled to the greatest extent possible in the light of experience and current technological knowledge. By inference, therefore, you are required to keep up to date with all relevant changes and/or developments within your area of work and responsibility.

Prescriptive legislation This is a term used to describe very detailed legislation, such as the Offices, Shops and Railway Premises Act 1963, which contains a list of legal do's and don't's. Modern legislation tends not to be prescriptive and instead defines general goals and standards to be achieved without detailing precisely how they are to be brought about.

Reasonably practicable This is the least strict duty and allows the cost in terms of money, time and effort to be weighed against the risk to be controlled – it might not be reasonably practicable to spend a lot of time, money and effort in controlling a small or insignificant risk. As the risk increases, so this argument decreases.

Regulations Regulations are secondary (subsidiary) pieces of legislation that are made under an Act. Regulations usually supplement the principles of their controlling (or enabling) Act but are more detailed and generally relate to a specific topic or hazard. For example, the Health and Safety at Work Act 1974, among other things, requires employers to ensure the safety of employees at work; by implication this includes those working with electricity. However, there are also Electricity at Work Regulations, made under the 1974 Act, that contain more detailed information on points to be considered when addressing electrical safety and fulfilling the general duty under the 1974 Act.

NOTE Regulations spelt with a capital 'R' refer to a complete set of Regulations (eg the Electricity at Work Regulations 1989). When an individual regulation within the set of Regulations is referred to, a lower case 'r' is used (eg regulation 7 of the Electricity at Work Regulations 1989).

Repeal and revoke As mentioned under 'Modified' (which see), it is sometimes necessary to amend existing legislation. In certain cases the existing legislation is so out of date that it is necessary to remove it altogether. When this removal involves an Act, the Act (or the specified sections of it) are said to be *repealed*. When the removal involves a set of Regulations (or specified individual regulations), the Regulations are said to be *revoked*.

Useful addresses

British Standards Institution (BSI)
Sales and Customer Services
389 Chiswick High Road
London W4 4AL

Tel: 0181-996 7000
Fax: 0181-996 7001

BSI Information Centre
Tel: 0181-996 7111
Fax: 0181-996 7048

Chartered Institute of Environmental Health (CIEH)
Chadwick Court
15 Hatfields
London SE1 8DJ

Tel: 0171-928 6006
Fax: 0171-827 5865

Community Transport Association (CTA)
London
A Block
211 Arlington Road
London NW1 7HD

Tel: 0171-284 4600
Fax: 0171-284 3279

Manchester
Highbank
Halton Street
Hyde
Cheshire SK14 2NY

Tel/Fax: 0161-351 1475
Tel/Fax: 0161-366 6685

Advice service
Tel/Fax: 0161-367 8780

HMSO
Enquiries: Tel: 0171-873 0011

Orders:
PO Box 276
London SW8 5DT

Tel: 0171-873 9090
Fax: 0171-873 8200

HSE Books
PO Box 1999
Sudbury
Suffolk CO10 6FS

Tel: 01787 881165
Fax: 01787 313995

HSE Information Centre
Broad Lane
Sheffield S3 7HQ

Tel: 0114-289 2345
Fax: 0114-289 2333

Local HSE offices, waste
regulation authorities, councils
and HMSO bookshops are listed
in the appropriate area
telephone directories.

Royal College of Nursing
20 Cavendish Square
London W1M 0AB

Tel: 0171-872 0840

About Age Concern

Health and Safety in Care Homes is one of a wide range of publications produced by Age Concern England, the National Council on Ageing. Age Concern England is actively engaged in training, information provision, fundraising and campaigning for retired people and those who work with them, and also in the provision of products and services such as insurance for older people.

A network of over 1,400 local Age Concern groups, with the support of around 250,000 volunteers, aims to improve the quality of life for older people and develop services appropriate to local needs and resources. These include advice and information, day care, visiting services, transport schemes, clubs, and specialist facilities for older people who are physically and mentally frail.

Age Concern England is a registered charity dependent on public support for the continuation and development of its work.

Age Concern England
1268 London Road
London SW16 4ER
Tel: 0181-679 8000

Age Concern Cymru
4th Floor
1 Cathedral Road
Cardiff CF1 9SD
Tel: 01222 371566

Age Concern Scotland
113 Rose Street
Edinburgh EH2 3DT
Tel: 0131-220 3345

Age Concern Northern Ireland
3 Lower Crescent
Belfast BT7 1NR
Tel: 01232 245729

Publications from ◆◆◆ Books

A wide range of titles is published by Age Concern England under the ACE Books imprint.

Good Care Management: A guide to setting up and managing a residential home

Jenyth Worsley

This companion volume to *Taking Good Care* has been written for care home proprietors and managers, present and prospective. Topics covered include setting up a home, contracts, budgetary planning, staff management and training, the management of care and quality control.

£10.99   0–86242–104–7

Business Skills for Care Management: A guide to costing, contracting and negotiating

Penny Mares

Negotiating contracts can be a time-consuming and complicated business for seasoned professionals. It can become a minefield for those with little direct experience in the area. Always practical and accessible, this easy-to-understand book for care managers guides the reader through all the key stages, always emphasising that the aim is to achieve the best quality service for users.

£10.99   0–86242–191–8

Expanding Care: A practical guide to diversification for care homes

Jenyth Worsley

This handbook outlines some of the ways in which care homes can diversify their activities – including the provision of domiciliary, day and respite care. It offers advice on assessing local needs, marketing and tendering, and explores the practical arrangements of implementation.

£14.95   0–86242–154–3

Health Care in Residential Homes
Dr Anne Roberts
Written in response to widespread demand for a book on this subject, *Health Care in Residential Homes* provides clear and straightforward information for managers and other care staff on maintaining residents' health and dealing with their health problems. Topics covered include the common illnesses of later life, the medicines prescribed, health promotion, what to do in an emergency, and coping with terminal illness and bereavement.

£14.95   0–86242–156–X

Dementia Care: A handbook for use in residential and day care
Alan Chapman, Alan Jacques and Mary Marshall
The number of dementia sufferers requiring care is increasing continuously. This practical guide for professional carers offers an understanding of the condition and provides advice on such issues as daily care, health maintenance, home design and staffing strategies.

£10.99   0–86242–128–4

Reminiscence and Recall: A guide to good practice
Faith Gibson
Reminiscence work is acknowledged as a successful therapy in the care of older people. This guide provides practical advice on planning and running reminiscence activity in a residential or day care setting and examines suitable approaches for people with particular conditions.

£10.99   0–86242–142–X

Residents' Money: A guide to good practice in care homes
People who live in a residential or nursing home have the same right as everyone else to spend their own money as they wish. This book sets out the basic principles involved in enabling older people to manage their own money and make their own choices.

£6.95   0–86242–205–1

If you would like to order any of these titles, please write to the address below, enclosing a cheque or money order for the appropriate amount made payable to Age Concern England. Credit card orders may be made on 0181-679 8000.

Mail Order Unit
Age Concern England
PO Box 9
London SW16 4ER

INFORMATION FACTSHEETS

Age Concern England produces over 30 Factsheets on a variety of subjects. Among these the following titles may be of interest to readers of this book:

10 *Local authority charging procedures for residential and nursing home care*

11 *Preserved rights to Income Support for residential and nursing homes*

22 *Legal arrangements for managing financial affairs*

Single copies are available free on receipt of a 9″ × 6″ stamped addressed envelope. If you require a selection of factsheets or multiple copies totalling more than five, charges will be given on request.

A complete set of factsheets is available in a ring binder at the current cost of £36, which includes the first year's subscription. The current cost for annual subscription for subsequent years is £17. There are different rates of subscription for people living abroad.

Factsheets are revised and updated throughout the year, and membership of the subscription service will ensure that your information is always current.

For a free list of all factsheets, or to order copies, send a large sae to:

Information and Policy Department
Age Concern England
1268 London Road
London SW16 4ER

Index